My Father, My Friend

My Father, My Friend

Arthur Mayse

Edited with an Afterword by Susan Mayse

Harbour Publishing

Harbour Publishing
Box 219
Madeira Park, BC V0N 2H0

Cover painting and drawings by Gaye Hammond.
Cover design by Roger Handling.

Printed and bound in Canada by Friesen Printers.

Canadian Cataloguing in Publication Data
  Mayse, Arthur, 1912-1992
    My father, my friend

  ISBN 1-55017-086-4

    1. Mayse, Arthur, 1912-1992 — Family. 2. Mayse, Amos William.
  3. Fly fishing — British Columbia — Vancouver Island.
  4. Fishers — British Columbia — Biography. I. Title.
  SH415.M39A3 1993.   799.1'2'092   C93-091353-1

Table of Contents

Acknowledgements

BILL AND WIN MAYSE'S FRIENDS made possible the release of *My Father, My Friend*. My special thanks to Brian Bolton, George Brandak, Kay and Terry Chettleburgh, Michael Clare, Margo Cormack, Humphrey Davy, Van Egan, Nick and Joy Golinski, Georgie Haugan, Mark Hume, Joan Munro, Elsie Norman, the Reverend Peter Parker, Jay Stewart, Jeanette Taylor, Howard White; Bill's sister Shirley Mayse, whose keen memory saved the day; Win's sisters Hazel Lyons, Mildred Rawson, Gladys Chambers; her nephew's widow Marquita Chambers; and all the loyal readers who have waited patiently for this book.

Bill and Win Mayse's personal and professional papers are now in the collections of the Campbell River Museum and Archives and the University of British Columbia Special Collections Library. Much of their trout and salmon fishing gear, including the classic Hardy rods which gave them a lifetime of pleasure, is now part of the sport fishing collection of the Campbell River Museum and Archives.

All proceeds from the sale of *My Father, My Friend* will go toward the important work of the Oyster River Enhancement Society, a non-profit organization created to protect and enhance the river's streambed, fish populations and nearby parklands. Individual donations to aid the society in its work are also welcome, and can be sent to:

Oyster River Enhancement Society
PO Box 93
Black Creek
British Columbia V0R 1C0

— *Susan Mayse*

1.

In The Beginning

LATE AT NIGHT AND WAKEFUL, I don't count sheep as some do. I have another approach. I fish a reach of my river, a Vancouver Island stream born in mountain country that drops by way of riffles and pools and freshet-carved bars to a Strait of Georgia forty miles away.

One of the loveliest waters that the good Lord ever laid down to delight an angler's heart, my river carries a prosaic name: the Oyster River. Far out on its estuary flats on a low-low tide, a man could treat himself to a dozen of the fine-flavoured little Olympia oysters now so rare on our Pacific coast.

I came to the Oyster as a boy after an apprenticeship in lesser waters. We lived in those years in Nanaimo, the tough and feisty British Columbia mining town to which my pastor father had brought us from Manitoba prairies, fishless except for suckers and whiskery bullheads. To me, eleven years old and sheltered as I'd been by my mother through years when my father was at war, all was new and strange and disconcerting.

On my first day at a Nanaimo school, I was plunged into my first fight. I was walking home with a straggle of other kids along the Esquimalt & Nanaimo railway tracks when half a dozen boys overtook us. They closed around me. One of them, a redhead freckled as a trout and no more than shoulder-high to me, gave me a violent shove.

I staggered, and came out with a startled, "Hey!"

"You looking for a fight?" the redhead demanded.

"No," I said. "Anyway, you're too little."

At that, the boy reached up and popped me on my nose. Blood flowed, but there was no time or chance for mopping up. The redhead was all over me, his hard fists thumping my ribs and lumping my face.

"Scrap—! scrap—!" The other boys and a few girls who had turned back to watch the diversion gave tongue in what was to become a too-familiar chant.

My craven instincts urged me to run. But sufficient sense remained in my rattled wits to warn me that the boy who ran from a fight would be an outcast forever after.

So I swung back awkwardly and blindly. It went on like that, the redhead peppering me with punches while I did my best to reciprocate. Twice I landed a fist with a satisfying smack. Encouraged, I waded in and stopped another solid clout with my nose. The fight continued until we were both staggering from weariness. At that point one of the older boys, the tough son of a Welsh coal miner, shoved between us.

"Okay," he said, "now you better shake hands."

We shook, grudgingly. I noted with satisfaction that the redhead hadn't come entirely unmarked from the encounter. He had a scrape on one cheekbone and a cut lip. His name was Tim O'Neil. Later, in a brittle sort of way, we became friends.

I took my bruised ribs and sore face home to the tree-shaded house on Milton Street where we lived. On the way, I paused to dab ditchwater ineffectually on my blood-splotched shirt, hoping that my mother would be out when I checked in.

I found my Dad toiling at what was to become one of his perennial projects. The Reverend Amos William Mayse, newly appointed pastor of Nanaimo's First Baptist Church, was swinging a sledgehammer against a boulder which humped its upper portion from the weedy grass plot that passed for a lawn. His shirt was open most of the way to his belly. His sleeves were rolled up past the biceps of his muscular, tattooed arms. His black hair was tousled, and he looked more like a labourer than a gentleman of the cloth.

Let me tell you a little about this man, since he is one with my river in memory. Of rather less than middle height, he was broad-built and stocky. Face and arms carried the indelible tan burned into them by the fierce South African sun. He was a veteran of two wars, the Boer War and the First World War. The second he had entered as an infantry private among his parishioners, not as a chaplain; he scorned to enlist in a non-combatant role.

I had been terrified of this man with the shiny black boots and the flared sergeant's stripes when he came home from the First World War to the cottage in Winnipeg's Fort Rouge district where my mother, older sister Shirley and I waited for him. He had grown himself a big sweeping moustache which made him all the more terrifying. But my father made short work of that unease. He picked me up and plunked me down in my little red wagon, which he towed with military strides down the street to a store with a windowful of fireworks stocked for Canada's Twenty-Fourth of May celebration. Dad bought out the window. Before that night's shoot-off ended, he stood somewhat higher in my estimation than the Almighty.

Dad grounded his sledge and gave me a long considering look. Then his square face with the shrapnel cleft in the chin cracked in a smile.

"Where's Ma?" I asked.

"Ladies' Aid," Dad told me. "Better get cleaned up before she comes home." And as an afterthought as I turned away, "You might as well burn that shirt."

He followed me indoors. While I splashed about in the bathroom, I could hear him rattling chairs in the kitchen. On the kitchen table when I came out, I saw a large old fishing creel. It was made of split willow that had once been varnished. The lid was buckled shut.

Dad set two mugs of sugared tea on the table.

"I don't know what's in that basket," he said. "I picked it up sight unseen at an estate auction this afternoon." His grin lightened his face. "Got it for two dollars. I thought we'd open it together."

Dad unbuckled the creel. He upended it on the table oilcloth. We stood gazing down at peculiar treasure. There was a fat flybook of shiny worn leather, its felt leaves gay as so many little gardens with their multiplicity of trout flies whipped to silkworm-gut snells. There was a Hardy Uniqua flyreel silvery from long use. Spooled on it was an enamelled flyline of black-and-white braided silk. A flat round aluminum tin held leaders, the used ones neatly coiled, the new ones still in their crackling isinglass envelopes. Add split shot for sinkers, spinners of shiny nickel and tarnished brass and copper, several cards of hooks tied to gut, and the trove was all but accounted for.

One item remained, a stubby brier pipe with silver-banded stem and blackened bowl. My father picked up the pipe, sniffed it, inspected it from all angles, then dropped it into his pocket. For years on our fishing jaunts, that pipe gripped between his teeth was as much a fixture as rod and creel.

"I'd like to have bid on the rods, too," Dad said, "but they were gone before I got there."

A block from our house, Milton Street ended at the Island Highway in those days, and across the highway lay a sizeable woodland tract then called Millstream Park. This park, un-pruned and untended, was heavily treed with cedar, ridge-barked Douglas fir, copper-limbed arbutus and dogwood that frothed white in the spring. Through the park wandered a picture-book stream that chattered from one rock-bound pool to another. Those pools sheltered native cutthroat trout, lively little fish that rarely exceeded ten inches in length.

It was here in the Millstream that my father and I were introduced, or rather introduced ourselves, to the sovereign sport and absorbing art of trout fishing.

As a boy in the English Midlands city of Sheffield, my father had gone into the coal mines at the age of twelve. Whenever he could manage it of a Saturday, he would board one of the crowded fishing trains that left the city's smoke and grime to drop their angler-passengers by canals and river reaches. Here they would set up their big green umbrellas for shade or shelter as the need might be, and dangle maggot-baited hooks for such coarse fish as roach and bream. Trout were not part of the working class angler's equation. Trout streams were, as they still are in England, reserved for the moneyed gentry who could pay for fishing privileges on a stretch of trout-bearing stream. That or, if their fortunes ran to it, purchase a riverside estate.

When he emigrated to Canada as a hand on a cattle boat

after the Boer War, my father could never quite believe that trout fishing in the Canadian West was free to anyone who could ply a rod. This feeling stuck with him in lesser degree all through his fishing years. He felt himself incredibly lucky to enjoy the freedom of the rivers.

In our Millstream fishing, my father handled the telescoping steel pole which was our only rod, and I was his faithful shadow. Once in a while, though, when he had taken time out to load his pipe or to empty the water from his leaky waders, Dad would grant me the privilege of holding the rod.

One chilly March day of high water and whipping wind, I dropped a hook baited with a gob of preserved salmon roe into a murky run. There was a brisk tug. I heaved back, and a silvery trout arced from its element into the stream-bordering greenery. I scrabbled for it, desperately afraid that it might slither back into the pool. But it didn't, and with its nine inches of speckle-and-silver in my hands, I knew that I was hooked no less securely than my little cutthroat had been. From that day I was a confirmed trout fisherman, prey to all the foibles and fancies, hopes and tribulations of the breed.

For the next year, the Millstream was our fishing world. Sometimes we fished it in open fields well out beyond the Nanaimo golf course, sometimes in its seaward reach where rise-dimpled evening water lay silver between the rotting wood-piles of an abandoned lumber yard. I fished in bib overalls, accepting wet feet and legs as the price of a day's outing. For some time, my father fished in his prim black baptistry waders, narrow-legged clerical jobs that gave his lower portion a peculiarly elfin appearance. Then at another auction he picked up a pair of much-patched Scottish waders, chest-high and a violent yellow in colour. These served him equally for fishing and, when the shoddy clerical pair gave out, for the rite of baptism, only partially masked by his sober black jacket.

Dad's salary was minuscule, and he had a family of four to

house, clothe and feed. By scrimping for a year Dad managed to save the price of a decent flyrod. Then, on the day we blundered into the local game warden, he came within a whisker of losing his stake. The warden asked to see our catch. Dad laid it out for him — seven trout ranging in size from ten to seven inches. The warden tapped the three smallest fish.

"Undersized," he said. "The limit is eight inches. Those could cost you ten bucks each."

"I didn't know there was a size limit," Dad said. "I should have, and I'm sorry."

The warden gave us a long, considering stare. "Watch it after this," he said.

He resumed his patrol. Dad let his breath out in a sigh of relief. It was a case where mercy paid off. We boned up on the fishing regulations, and abode by them strictly for all the years of our fishing together.

Dad bought his new rod, a Milward of sound English construction. I was with him in a Nanaimo sporting goods store the day he bought it. Vividly as if it were yesterday, I remember watching him slide its gleaming split cane sections from their cotton bag, and the smile that kindled his square-built face as he fitted them together. We admired the rod. Then Dad took his old steel telescoping rod from the hall closet and placed it in my hands.

"Yours," he said. And so it remained until I aspired to a flyrod of my own.

About this time too we acquired a secondhand Model-T Ford. Our horizons expanded. We ventured as far south as the Cowichan River, and north even to that tributary of the brawling Campbell called the Quinsam.

Then one night as we churned our way at twenty-five miles an hour along a gravelled Island Highway fifteen miles north of Courtenay, our headlights blinked out. This happened with some regularity. Trudging ahead with a flashlight, I guided Dad into a little roadside park heavily shaded by dim-seen old maple and alder trees. By the flashlight's weak beam, we pitched our tent.

The last sound in my ears as I dropped off to sleep was the murmur of running water. I didn't know it then, but my fortunes had brought me to the river which was to become one of my life's dearest loves.

2.

Downriver

At our first meeting, my feelings for the river were ambivalent. I liked the sparkle and busy chatter of its riffles, but wading them promised to be a sterner challenge than my splashing around in the little Millstream. The alder-shaded pools, green and mysterious in their deeps, crystal clear where they shallowed to exit runs paved with golden gravel, were fair to the eye but far bigger than I was used to. How could I fish them with gear that limited each cast to fifteen, or at full stretch, maybe twenty feet?

On this our first day, though, we were not to fish in the river proper.

"The place to catch trout," said the British Columbia Forest Service man in charge of the park where we'd put in, "is right down at the river mouth. What you do is get there a little before low tide and fish the rise." He sized me up — faded overalls, steel rod and cheap tin reel — and his fire-scarred face eased into a grin.

"Expect you'll need bait," the warden said. "You can take my spade and turn up some worms in that marshy spot across by the spring."

Worms we did not need, though. We had brought our own from the wormery my father maintained with loving care in a corner of his vegetable garden. It was my job to spade the garden, turning up its rich, dark soil in the rows where carrots and onions, peas and potatoes, would flourish. Worms showed in each spadeful, but I was under orders not to take them all.

"Leave half of them," my father told me. "There's nothing better for a garden than plenty of worms."

Those destined for fish bait, I dropped wriggling into a can. At the end of each spading session, I took the can down to the old washtub which was my father's worm farm. Another of my chores was to collect any bakery wagon, vegetable van or milk delivery horse droppings deposited along our block. Into his worm farm's manure-fortified earth Dad would mix carefully measured portions of cornmeal, molasses and coffee grounds. Then we would dump in our take of worms and cover the tub with moss fetched home from the woods. Even those crawlers that were scrawny and anaemic when they went into the tub emerged plump and fighting fit. Their diet turned them a healthy pink shading into grey. They were lively. They squirmed like mad when strung on a hook. The little resident trout of the Millstream couldn't resist them.

We had stowed a lard pail of those high-conditioned worms in the back of the Model-T. With filled bait cans and the warden's directions to guide us, we set out for the river mouth. First we crossed the river by a humpbacked wooden bridge weathered to silver grey. This with a pause for a ritual scan of the pool below to see if any trout lurked at its tail. Then on, to turn seaward from the highway into a narrow earth road that wound across a field and past a one-room white schoolhouse.

Below the school, the road narrowed into a trail traversing a grassy glade where enormous broadleaved maples unfurled their green canopies. The trail skirted the split-rail fence of a farm. It passed close by a sheep shed. The sheep, according to local legend, had been raided by wolves, and certainly the grim litter of bleached bones and torn fleeces gave evidence that mayhem and murder had been committed here. The work was probably that of a dog pack, scourge of every sheep farmer. But wolves made a better story. From there, the trail crossed a sea-oats swamp by way of a rotting log deposited by some mighty winter tide. Beyond were the salt grass and whitened driftwood, the stony plains and the wide emptiness of the river estuary.

It occurred to me as we tramped out across the river-mouth flats that this was a mighty strange place to expect trout. Cutthroat, after all, were denizens of pool and shady reach, not of a characterless and hostile tideflat. To underline this hostility, a little grey black-spotted snake glided from the shelter of a saltgrass clump, arranged itself in as much of a coil as its one-foot length could manage, and feinted a strike at my running shoe. Even though I knew the snake was harmless, nothing more than a bad-tempered wandering garter snake, I got the message. This was no place for humans. We were not welcome here.

I had a strong urge to point this out to my father, to suggest we turn back to the friendlier upstream reaches. But he was tramping along sturdily in his patched yellow waders, rod nodding in his hand and a wisp of smoke trailing back from his pipe, and I found the sight reassuring. If he wasn't bothered, I wouldn't be either.

The Oyster was a beautiful river, I later came to realize, certainly the most beautiful river I've ever seen. It was absolutely pristine. There were fine timber stands in the upper waters and they controlled the flow. It sheltered a good run of searun cutthroat trout—always my favourite sport fish—and several species of salmon. It was the most idyllic fly fisherman's river on Vancouver Island.

We came to a channel that flowed strong and silent over rounded stones from which trailed skeins of brown seaweed. The effect was sinister, but my father splashed in and forged across. I followed, shrinking at the bite of cold water through runners and overalls. My imagination, always too vivid, turned the streaming brown weed to dead women's hair, and peopled the dark flow with monsters.

This was a mere side channel. We crunched across a bar of water-smoothed stones and, of a sudden, there was the true river. It eddied lazily down a widening reach. Out beyond a long-snouted bar where seagulls squatted by the hundred, it lost itself in the salt water of the Strait of Georgia.

Dad waded in hip deep. He extracted a worm from the can clipped to his waders belt and baited up. Then he commenced the monotonous routine of slinging a worm-baited spinner into the lazy flowage and recovering it in a series of unhurried pulls.

My father, though a mighty fisher before the Lord, never did aspire to become a fly fisherman. All his life long, he stuck to his spinner with trailing gut-hook and worm impaled. This he handled with telling effect and with a long enduring patience that his grasshopper son could only envy. It would surprise me not at all to learn that he fishes a river of Paradise these days, with a solid gold spinner and celestial worm.

Bored, sprawled on the sunwarmed bar, I watched him. Once it seemed to me that his rod checked and took on a sudden bend. But nothing transpired, and I decided that the hiatus had been no more than a pause to rest his arm.

He was a simple man, my father. At sixteen, he added a couple of years to his age and enlisted in the York and Lancaster Regiment—the Royal Tigers, he called them proudly—and was shipped overseas to South Africa and the Boer War. In the course of time his affinity for the wide and lonely veldt won him a place as a mounted scout for his column. As such he might ride alone half a day's march ahead of the regiment.

Once, as Dad told me the tale over a campfire, he was skirting one of the rocky hills that the Boers called kopjes when a bullet clipped across his saddle bow. With the rifle report still in his ears, he dropped off his horse into high grass. The horse, a well-salted Argentine, would stand until he returned for it, if he was that lucky. Trailing his Lee-Metford, he crept through grass to the kopje. He started up, rifle ready. Another shot spanged into the rock inches from his head; he changed direction, flanking and working his way above the area from which the shot had been fired. Cautiously, he poked his head between boulders and looked down. Scarce twenty-five feet below him, he saw a sky-blue backside nestled between rocks.

My father snuggled his rifle to his shoulder. But something about that broad Dutch butt caused him to shift his aim. He fired into empty air. The Boer backed out of his crevice, lunged to his feet and whirled with rifle ready. My father got up too. They faced each other, enemies, men whose duty was to kill each other. Then they both began to laugh. They were boys, the young Boer no older than my father.

They sat down together. My father offered a can of bully beef and some hardtack biscuits from his haversack. The Boer brought out peaches from his family's farm and a twist of strong black tobacco. They ate and they smoked, and at the end, in laboured English, the Boer issued an invitation.

When the war ended, my father would be welcome on the farm where the peaches grew. A place and a job would be found for him there. As my father remembered it, his name was Piet

von Troikker. They shook hands, slung their rifles and went their separate ways.

Soon afterward my father was wounded in arms, legs and jaw by a shrapnel burst, and taken prisoner. Released from a Boer prison camp by General Jan Smuts — he was slowly starving because he was unable to eat the Boers' coarse mealie corn with a broken jaw — and invalided home to England, my father thought long and hard about that offer of a new life in a spacious land. England now seemed too narrow and grey. But he'd had enough of Africa, and he could work his passage on a cattle boat to Canada. He never mentioned his meeting with the young Boer in his terse diary; if he'd been caught at the time fraternizing with the enemy he would have been shot for treason.

When he first came out my father worked as a rough carpenter, since he had always been good with his hands. Then, having decided that his mission was to serve his God — he had been a Methodist hedge preacher in his teens — he talked his way into a prairie Baptist theological college where a young man of scant education but great earnestness could find a berth.

Ordained and married, he went as a missioner to the Peguis Indian Reserve on Manitoba's Red River. I was born there among the Swampy Cree. Since my mother was ailing and I was sickly I had a nurse; my survival depended on Maggie Flett, a Scots-Cree Métis woman who treated me as her own child in every way. As a baby I dangled in a mossbag from a tree bough with Indian babies for company. My first memory is of lying in long grass, seeing an older boy holding up his bow and a bright-feathered duck so I could admire his first kill. My first shoes were beaded buckskin moccasins, my first meat bearpaw and beavertail.

Dad's yell came loud and clear across the Oyster mouth. He was out waist-deep now, and his rod was bowed in a glorious arc. Foot by foot he backed ashore, towing a fish that splashed and flurried and once flung itself gleaming a yard into the air. My father skidded it up the shingle, where I pounced on it.

I'd been wrong. This indeed was trout water, and our little Millstream had never yielded such a trout as this! It was our first example of the searun cutthroat, and we gloated over it.

It seemed to me, crouched on the bar and gazing down at my Dad's firstling, that I had never seen any creature so beautiful. Its underbelly was clean white, set off by paired orange pectoral fins. Its sides shaded from silver to a bronze lavishly peppered with black speckles shaped like little Maltese crosses. The broad square-cut tail was also spotted. The back was olive and the flanks were burnished to a golden sheen. I took in its stream-moulded shape and its neat predator's head and was consumed by a yearning to catch just such a wonder-fish for myself.

Dad swathed his trout in a wrapping of brown kelp leaf and laid it in the lee of piled stones that would mark its place and keep it shaded. Then he draped his hook with another of his super-worms and waded out from the bar. I followed him, stepping carefully, still a little afraid of the wide water. When I was in past my knees, I pulled line from my reel and lobbed out a clumsy cast.

The sun climbed higher. Drugged by the monotony of cast and recover, and with no expectation of hooking a fish, I let my eyes and my thoughts wander. Seagulls took to the air in a white blizzard from one of the outer bars that guarded the river mouth. Across on the timbered point that bounded the estuary to the north, a pair of bald eagles lorded it high in a fir tree, their snowy necks and heads shining in the sun. A pair of mallards planed in and power-stalled to a landing in the cross-stream shallows . . .

A hard and sudden tug jerked the line out of my fingers. I hauled back and met a live and stubborn resistance. My steel rod creaked; its tip strained over.

This was no Millstream tiddler to be yoicked from the stream and tossed over my head to the shore! We tussled for what seemed an interminable time, the trout whipsawing this way and that, me floundering toward the bar. Twice my searun cutthroat leaped, bringing my heart into my throat each time. Then it was weaving and swirling in shallow water.

I drew it flapping and bouncing up the bar. Midway up the slope, the hook lost its hold. Freed, my trout began to skitter back toward the water. I dropped my rod and fell on the cutty. From that position, hugging my prize, I looked up at a pair of wader legs no less patched than my father's.

A deep voice with an upward lilt in it said, "You'll squeeze the guts out of him, boy."

I scrambled to my feet, trout still clutched against my chest. The pair who had arrived on the scene were brown of face and lean of build. Both were smiling. Their jackets, relics of ancient suits worn over heavy wool shirts, were shiny-drab. They looked nondescript and river-wise as two fishing herons. The reels they carried had the same worn-metal shine as dad's old Uniqua, and the long, heavy rods grounded at their feet were not of cane but of some dark wood. Later I learned they were Welsh coal miners from the inland town of Cumberland a few miles southwest. Fishing was their passion, one which they indulged whenever a free Saturday came their way. Waddy Williams and Dick James, their names were. A year or two later, Dick James went out of his way to make me a gift of fishing knowledge for which I have always been grateful.

Their rods were made of greenheart, a dense, heavy, resilient wood. The joints were spliced together; instead of slipping metal ferrules together, fishermen had to wrap the joint with cord or tape. Greenheart—which really predated split bamboo—made a good rod, but as heavy as sin. There were some master casters among the miners, despite miserably inadequate lines. Those were the years of the enamelled silk line; the modern vacuum-dressed nylon lines were unknown then. They could lay a very nice fly with that relatively crude equipment.

The two miners left me to commune with my fish, wading

far out from the bar with vigorous surges. On station, they began to cast. They were fishing with flies, a departure I had never before witnessed, and it seemed to me that those flies sailed out for an incredible distance.

The trout—my trout—was an inch or so shorter than my father's but deeper in body and no less beautiful. I wrapped it in seaweed and laid it by the other, and the process that had started with my first Millstream trout was all but complete.

Fishing had become more than a pastime to me. It was a way of life, a pursuit to be dreamed of during the dark days of winter and indulged on all possible occasions when the winds blew warm and the stream-loving alders leafed out.

Nor did those searun cutties, our first from the Oyster, render up their lives in vain. Under my father's instructions, I built a fire under the iron grate in our camp fireplace, starting it with cedar and bringing it to the required bed of coals with nubbins of Douglas fir bark. Dad laid our trout, cleaned and beheaded, rolled in cornmeal and with a rasher of bacon in each body cavity, in the big cast-iron frying pan brought from home. He set potatoes on to boil in their jackets in a billy can and opened a tin of peas. The trout came from the fire with skins crisped to a dark brown. Their sides, pink and steaming, peeled away from their backbones. A whiff of pepper, a touch of salt and they were ready for our plates. We sat on log ends by our dying fire and wolfed our dinner down. Always before I'd turned up my nose at fish. But those trout gave eating a new dimension. They were not merely good; they were superlative. They made a meal not to be forgotten, which we devoured by the fire with the river song gentle in our ears.

3.

The MacEevor

ONE DAY, OUT OF CURIOSITY, Dad and I walked up to investigate the shake roof of a sturdy log cabin showing over a fold in the wild pasture that rolled down to the foreshore north of the Oyster River estuary. No smoke curled from its stovepipe chimney. Whoever the owner might be, he wasn't at home. The cabin was built of broad-axed logs, its squared timbers fitted so precisely that only a narrow chinking of moss-and-clay amalgam showed between courses. Spiked above the split log door was a pair of elk horns.

A dirt-crusted window offered a dim view of the cabin's single room. Apart from a stove in a sand-filled crib, the place boasted only a driftwood plank table and a bunk in which were tumbled what looked like rolls of gunnysacking. Back of the cabin was a small shake barn from which a horse whinnied as we passed. There was no sign of truck, car or powered machinery. A weatherbeaten wagon poked its shafts skyward from the barnyard, and a few scrawny hens pecked and scurried around a stoneboat canted on one side.

We enquired at Fishermen's Lodge, the hotel on the north bank of the river, about the cabin. It belonged to James MacIvor, we were told by Ma Taylor, and we'd do well to keep away from it and him. Nobody knew for sure, because people didn't stray down there, but the rumour was that the owner discouraged trespassers with traps and spring-guns. MacIvor was the original old man of the river, eccentric and hostile. Nobody knew much about him, except that he'd been squatting down there since Kingdom Come.

Then, a few days later, we got our first glimpse of MacIvor.

We had been fishing upriver and were heading for camp along what had once been the mainline of a logging railroad when a thunder of hooves and a shrill yelping assaulted our ears. Alarmed, we pulled over to the side of the grade. A mob of cattle tore past us, running all out. They were big old steers, mossy-horned and wild-eyed. Pounding along behind the steers came a man almost as wild and unkempt as his beasts. He was closer to seven feet than six. Grey shoulder-long hair streamed in the breeze. His pants were patched at knees and seat. He was bare to the waist, and his chest sported a mat of coarse grey hair. At his heels loped a black dog that appeared to be more wolf than canine.

Steers, man and dog rushed past us in a boil of dust. We looked at each other.

"You know," Dad said, "I think maybe that was old MacIvor."

MacIvor it was, hazing a bunch of his beef cattle home from their upriver range to his corral. The next time we saw the formidable old man, he was lounging with rump propped

against a campsite table in the forestry park. He was scowling over an old Vancouver newspaper fished from a trash can.

"Murderin's and killin's," he rumbled as we came up to him from the river. "That's all they have over there." He lowered his paper. Fierce blue eyes regarded us from under shaggy brows. "I only went there once. I got robbed." Then, abruptly to my father, "What's your name, Mister?"

In the days and years that followed, we came to know this hermit of Oyster River as a friend. He was a Cape Breton Scot, he told us once, the three of us sitting on a beach log and he in discursive mood. An itchy foot had brought him west to California. In San Francisco, word came to his ears of a spectacular gold strike in British Columbia.

MacIvor — he called himself "The MacEevor" as befitted the laird of his half-wild acres — had invested his savings in a sloop-rigged thirty-footer, a craft which a man alone could handle. With stores for his journey on board, he had beaten his way along the wild and hostile North Pacific coast until a vicious storm swooped down on him near the top of the Strait of Georgia. He was running before the gale, mast bare except for a scrap of driver sail, when he fell foul of the bars that lie in wait off the mouth of the Oyster.

He cleared one bar only to be hurled on another. He found himself swimming for his life, sloop gone with the bottom bashed out of her. The sloop's mast, wave tossed, came within reach. MacIvor hooked an arm around it and clung until, bruised and logey with salt water taken, he was washed ashore. He had the clothes he stood in and a few silver dollars in his pocket, nothing more. There was no sign of habitation. The woods stretched unbroken except where the river coiled down to the hostile sea.

Miles to the south, MacIvor had noted smoke from what he took to be an Indian encampment. He swam the river mouth and set out along the beaches in that direction; there would be no road for many years. When creeks barred his way, he forded or swam them. Finally, with darkness closing in, he arrived at the source of the smoke. It was a settler's cabin.

The settler provided MacIvor with matches and a spare axe, for which he insisted on paying with his silver dollars, and offered him shelter for the night. But MacIvor declined the invitation. Axe on shoulder, matches wrapped in a scrap of oilskin, he set off for the spot miles north where the storm had hurled him ashore. Gold rush be damned! He liked the look of the land: here was where he would make his home.

And so he did. By labour infinite, he pushed the woods back, burning and uprooting until he had wrestled a field from a land where all was untamed. Other settlers filtered in, but MacIvor, a solitary man by nature, kept to himself. There he stayed in his cabin above the beach, the mast that saved him propped on a couple of logs out front, leaving his land only when necessity demanded.

One of those necessities arose when the bodies of seven French sailors, less lucky than MacIvor had been, washed ashore after a gale wrecked their barque. The thought of laying them away without Christian burial went against MacIvor's conscience. So he draped a poor drowned seaman across each shoulder and, travelling by beaches and forest trails, packed them twenty miles south to the settlement of Comox. He then returned for two more bodies, and another two after that. His final trek was easier: he had but one corpse to carry. Their gravestone stood for years at the foot of Courtenay's Mission Hill.

Even in old age, MacIvor remained a man of giant strength who could handle two men's work, as he proved when it came time to span the Oyster with a bridge. Hired to help with the project, he would pick up one end of a massive timber and, while two lesser men struggled with the other end, heave it into position. He drew two men's wages on that job, MacIvor told us proudly, and I have no doubt he earned them.

One day when Dad and I were fishing the estuary, MacIvor strolled down to watch. He was dripping wet: an iron man impervious to weather, he was fresh from his daily swim in the saltchuck—a dunking for which he never bothered to shed his clothes. Unimpressed, MacIvor watched us take a brace of nice searuns. In his early years on the river, he told us, when it was live off the land or go hungry, he had gone after these little speckled fish, these trouts. His tackle had consisted of an alder pole rigged with a length of haywire for line, and a cod hook baited with any scrap of fish or meat he could come by.

"Used to catch 'em by the dozen," he said. "Lot bigger'n these of yours, too. Salted 'em down in a barrel."

Once MacIvor invited us to his cabin for a meal. Dad hesitated, but only for an instant.

"Be honoured, Mac," he said, and up to the cabin we trudged with MacIvor stumping ahead of us. "Got bread," he said as we disposed ourselves on the crates that served as chairs, "and there's a bit of meat around somewhere."

"That's fine," Dad said, "but what I'd really like is a boiled egg."

"Me, too," I piped up, grateful to my father for the inspiration. At least an egg protected by its shell seemed a safer collation than meat of dubious age and condition.

While we ate our eggs and sipped our heavily sugared black tea, MacIvor told us how once when cash was scarce and expenses heavy, he had decided to sell some of the timber off his wooded acres. A deal was made. The loggers moved in. But MacIvor didn't cotton to the way they were knocking down trees—his trees—indiscriminately with their steam-powered steel lines. He ordered them off his land. The loggers refused to clear out. For answer, MacIvor loaded his .30-.30 and descended on them with fire in his eye. He ran them off at rifle point, speeding their exodus with shots fired over their heads.

That caper fetched him a spell in the skookum-house, as the Chinook trade jargon styled it, but MacIvor remained stubbornly unrepentant.

"Jail wasn't anything," he said. "I just sat around and ate my fill at the King's expense. I'd do it again if I had to."

But the loggers wanted no further part of the forbidding giant with the drooping whiskers and the shock of yellow hair. His woods were left untouched as they largely remain, as a nature preserve, to this day.

MacIvor never married, although once late in life he tried, in the ancient way of the highland clans, to buy a girl from her father. He took a great fancy to thirteen-year-old Winifred Davey, visiting from Vancouver, and approached her father. Possibly his intent was to bring her along until she grew up, then marry her. Ernest Davey declined the offer. MacIvor's only known relative was a nephew who came out to stay with him once. MacIvor pointed to a pile of dirty old gunnysacks in the corner and said, "There's your bed, you can sleep there." According to the story, the nephew stayed one night and then got out as if the devil were after him.

In his later years, time worked its changes on MacIvor. His shoulders bowed, his barrel of a chest sank in. One bad spring, the wagonload of firewood he was bringing in overset on him, injuring a shoulder and breaking several ribs. MacIvor spent minimal time in hospital. Then, with ribs taped and arm in a sling, he hurried home to his river-mouth spread. His hurts were a long time mending. He was still under the weather when we looked in on him that September. MacIvor's hair was white by then; with his wild mane, he looked uncommonly like one of the doom-crying Old Testament prophets.

"I'll cut some stove wood for you, Mac," I offered as we concluded our meal of bread, boiled eggs and tea.

"Like hell you will!" MacIvor growled at me. It was plain that I had offended him. "I've cut my own firewood all my life and I don't mean to quit now."

James MacIvor lasted a year or two longer. Then he departed this life, and his woods and fields and lovely foreshore passed into other hands. Rumours that he had cached a fortune in gold around his cabin lured treasure-hunting trespassers until the ground around was pockmarked with holes. No hidden trove of gold coins was turned up.

Eventually someone torched his cabin. Its logs burned fiercely for a long time, lighting the night sky so that we could see the glare even from our camp upriver.

4.

The Fly Fishermen

Between pastoral calls and beating out sermon notes on his rickety old Oliver typewriter, my father toiled to restore our badly neglected yard to some semblance of order. He trimmed the over-long grass with a borrowed hand mower. Dad loved his garden, and he was a great gardener. His green thumb worked wonders with spindly shrubs and indifferent borders. At intervals too he would take sledge in hand and renew his attack on the massive boulder that humped its tip through our lawn.

One day he smote it so mighty a blow that his sledge handle broke. Dad was staring at the rock in controlled exasperation when our neighbour on the uphill side hailed him over the fence. Arthur Newbury was powder boss in one of Nanaimo's coal mines.

"Hey, Padre," he called, "why don't you let me blow that rock for you?"

My father took pride in doing for himself. But he was no explosives expert.

"Thanks, Art," he called back. "I won't take your time with that. But if I could find me a bit of powder and fuse, I'd like to have a go at it myself."

The powder boss obliged. He provided my father with two sticks of sixty percent dynamite, several feet of coiled white fuse, and a pair of dynamite caps. Also he supplied a lesson in the use of high explosives. When he had showed my father how to nip the cap on the fuse, then tuck it into a hole reamed in the side of a dynamite stick, he added a warning.

"Now look," he said. "You should find half a stick plenty. When you touch off the fuse, don't hang around. Run like— like—"

"Like hell," my father cheerfully supplied. He thanked the powder boss and stowed the blasting gear on a shelf in our garage.

One Saturday afternoon, following instructions with finicky care, my father cut one of the powder sticks in half with his jackknife, fitted fuse and dynamite cap, and nestled the charge in a hole scooped under the side of our mossy grey boulder.

Dad lit the fuse. We ran like hell.

Sheltered by the house corner, we waited for the explosion. When it came, it was disappointing—a minor *Whump!* followed by a patter of displaced gravel. We advanced on the boulder, peering at it through a drift of smoke. Its appearance hadn't changed. Except for a minor nick or two, it was as we'd last seen it.

"Guess it's not going to work," I said.

But my father was never one to give in easily.

"Next time," he said, "we'll make the charge bigger."

He went to the garage for a roll of electric tape. While I watched in dismay, he taped the half stick of powder to the remaining whole stick, and gouged a cavity for the dynamite cap.

"You think maybe that's too much powder, Dad?" I asked nervously.

"I just hope it's enough," he said.

He fitted the fused cap, tamped the mealy dynamite around it with his thumbs, and advanced on the rock. Charge laid, he whipped a kitchen match across his haunch, applied flame to fuse, and once more we fled. We were no sooner around the house corner than an echoing *BOOM!* made the air shiver. The blowup was followed by the tinkle of broken glass. As we ventured around the corner, my mother poked her head through a dining room window frame from which the panes had been removed.

"Will!" she cried to my father. "What on earth are you doing?"

The blast had also blown out dining room and kitchen windows in Art the powder boss's house. Art was very Christian about it, but he never offered to loan my father any more blasting powder. As for the rock, my father's bête noir, it had lost most of its moss but was still firmly in place. Forced finally to admit defeat, my father let the boulder alone thereafter. It still heaved its nose out of our lawn when we left that house to move to Vancouver. Dad compromised by filling the hollow crown of it with earth and planting it full of nasturtiums.

One evening around this time Dad announced that he had a call to make. "Deacon Coulter's girl has appendicitis. I have to persuade Coulter to put her in hospital."

When he returned from his call well on in the evening, he gave me a short answer when I asked about the afflicted girl. "She's in hospital," he said, "and none too soon."

I noticed that he was doing his best to keep his right hand out of sight. The knuckles were swollen and bruised.

The story leaked out, as leak it must in a small and gabby town.

My father had found the girl in a bad way, fevered and delirious. Her mother was in an agony of grief and worry, but the deacon retained an iron calm. "Get her to hospital," my father urged.

"That I will not," said the deacon. "If it is the Lord's will, the lass will get better. If not, blessed is the name of the Lord."

My father wasted no more time in persuasion.

"I'm taking her to hospital," he said, and started for the bed.

"You will not," said the deacon, interposing his considerable bulk between bed and pastor.

With that, my father drew back his right arm and clipped the deacon solidly on the angle of his jaw, stepped over his prone body and bundled the girl in a couple of blankets. With her in his arms, he again stepped over the deacon—now twitching and moaning as consciousness returned—and with the distraught mother tagging after, carried the appendicitis victim to his car. She arrived at the hospital in time to prevent her appendix from bursting, a catastrophe that could have meant peritonitis and a cruel death.

Deacon Coulter quit our church and took himself off to join a faith-healing sect, but my father's loss was also his gain.

The story spread. Next Sunday morning, a dozen strange faces looked toward the pulpit from the rearmost pew. The faces belonged to Welsh miners: scrubbed, coal dust reamed from under their fingernails, and turned out in their Sabbath best. Word of that life-saving clout had spread like wildfire. With those Welsh voices to give them substance, the hymns never sounded better.

Later, the regard the tough miners of Nanaimo had for my father was doubly cemented. One day the whistles on Protection Island began to blow the sequence that a mining community dreads to hear. *Accident,* they signalled. *Men hurt!* I still remember all the whistles blowing, and the terrible fear, almost panic, and tension and worry, that went through the town. Once those whistles all started blowing, we knew there had been a bad accident.

About two hours after the blast, when fumes were still drifting through the area, Dad crossed to Protection Island on a tugboat with a party of draegermen, rescuers from another mine who had hurried to lend a hand. My mother didn't want him to go, but he insisted. The draegermen saved most of the men trapped below by the gas explosion that fetched down a section of the drift's roof, but one they could not save. He lay pinned and hopelessly injured by a rock that couldn't be shifted.

My father went down to him in spite of all arguments and warnings. He prayed with the trapped miner while overhead the sagging roof grumbled ominously and sprayed the drift with overburden and lesser stones. He stayed with the man, holding his hand, until he died. They brought my father up the shaft with face blackened as any miner's and with tears cutting runnels in the coal dust.

Dad never exploited his own coal mine experience from the pulpit; it was just part of his past, something he took for granted. Normally the miners would have had little to do with a preacher, but they seemed to feel differently about him. He was a merry-hearted man. He could knock back a shot of rum, and he was extremely popular with men, especially with men of their hands.

He was always at his best with miners and loggers and fishermen.

Frequently we went on fishing trips with Nanaimo miners, who were great trout fishermen, to various lakes and streams. It was a great life for a boy. Very few of the miners aspired to Hardy tackle, because Hardy was the very expensive gentleman's fishing rod. Many of them would use an English Milward or a Scottish Sharp, a cut below Hardy.

Strangely, nobody bothered much with sport fishing for salmon or steelhead. Boats were hard to come by; this was long before the outboard motor and the fourteen-foot utility boat mounted on a trailer that you could launch anywhere. Dad was lucky. He knew a butcher, Mr. Growcott, who had a real drowner of a twenty-six-foot launch. We used to go out salmon fishing on that, usually to the Five Finger Islands off Nanaimo, but sometimes we ventured farther afield. Mr. Growcott, God bless him, was no sailor. On these trips I shuttled between delight and terror and sheer misery. Once we ventured down to Dodds Narrows, a fearsome place with whirlpools in all directions, and Mr. Growcott's launch lost its power in the middle of the worst passage of the Narrows. We went spinning in circles through them, riding the edge of whirlpools, and I really thought all was lost that day. That boat was a floating coffin, a far cry from the modern seaworthy boat. I look back at it now with horror.

My father's month-long annual vacation meant a month away from his pulpit. Substitute ministers would fill in for him, an amiable arrangement that served all parties. When one of his subs needed a Sunday off, my father would repay the favour by standing in for him.

This time when Dad and I headed north, I had my own flyrod. A year of saving my minuscule allowance and of gleaning sparse tips from travellers whose bags I ferried by coaster wagon from station to hotel made that longed-for purchase possible.

The rod cost twelve dollars. In my eyes, it was a thing of beauty with its varnished split cane sections, its cork-wrapped handle and its scarlet bindings. But let me point out now that the rod did not live up to its appearance. It was what fishermen contemptuously refer to as a buggy whip: a gutless nine feet of too-limber bamboo with which not even a tournament champion could lay out a long cast. But I loved it and endured its treacheries, reglueing its segments when the faithless stickum that bound them gave up the struggle. I also reattached ferrules that showed a distressing tendency to peel off, and replaced the pot metal guides and tip-top with a new set. For all its deficiencies, I still remember that rod with grudging fondness, for it was with it that I enticed my first trout to a cast fly.

This to-me earthshaking event took place on the lower river on a muggy, mothy evening when the sky over the western ranges was painted in sunset colours of rose and apple green. From the Willows pool at the last elbow above the saltchuck all the way down to the estuary stretched prime trout water. Tide-choked, it lay still and silvery in the gentle evening light, its surface marred only by the occasional rings of a rising fish. These were the same roistering searun cutthroat that we fished for at the river mouth. But on the rising tide, on a warm still evening, they mimicked the ways of their aristocratic cousins, the brown trout of such hallowed English waters as Test and Itchen. They rose daintily, fed selectively, and, for a frustrated boy doing his damnedest to propel a worm-and-spinner out to them, were impossible to catch.

As usual that evening, half a dozen anglers aware of this twilight invasion had sifted down from the highway. Spaced out along the reach, they plied their art with a skill that I could only envy. Occasionally one or other of them would sink hook in a trout, an event marked by a splash and a flirt of spray.

All present were fly fishermen — all except me — and I watched them with hopeless longing while I heaved out my damnation spinner.

Gravel crunched behind me where I stood on the shingle

bar groping another worm from my can. One of the fly fishermen stood there smiling at me. His hair was grey, and his spectacles gave off a phantom glimmer.

"Listen," he said, "when they're in like this, you'll get nowhere with a worm and spinner. How'd you like to try a fly?"

He pulled a flat aluminum flybox from his jacket, flipped back the lid and lifted a fly from one of the orderly rows.

"This is a Royal Coachman," he told me. "It might do the trick."

I cut the cumbersome worm and spinner rig from my leader, then watched while the grey-haired angler knotted on the fly. It dangled there, flaunting its paired white wings and red silk body double-banded with peacock herl.

"There," said my angel. "Now get in and give it a try."

He waded in beside me. Hand guiding my elbow, he gave me my first lesson in fly casting.

"Not too far back with the rod," he said. "Don't let it slant over your shoulder. Check your backcast so the line will have a chance to straighten out behind you. Then drive it forward."

His hand piloted me through the motions. Amazed, I watched my line reach out farther than it ever had before, to drop the fly on the glass-smooth surface.

"Now you try it by yourself," my mentor told me. "That's right—don't let it sag—"

He stayed with me for a quarter-hour, explaining and demonstrating. Then he waded off downstream to resume his own masterly laying-out of a fly.

It was now deep dusk. The sunset was fading. Nighthawks swooped low over the water in pursuit of insects, perhaps the same ones to which the occasional trout still rose. I sent out another cast, rejoicing in my newly acquired savvy. While the fly still floated, the water under it blossomed in a ghostly rosette. A brisk yank thrilled along the line to my fingers. Then I was tied to my first fly-hooked trout.

Doc Moore, my benefactor was. Besides being a master angler, he was a dentist in the town of Courtenay fifteen miles away. I honour his memory, for he did what most of us are too lazy or too preoccupied with our own affairs to do. He turned aside from his own sport to initiate a twelve-year-old boy into his craft and gentle art. For that, this man-once-boy will be forever thankful. May the rivers of Paradise run sweetly for him.

I had passed another milestone. I had become what I remain to this day, a convinced fly fisherman.

5.

A River Has Two Faces

I HAD MY NEW FLYROD, but my reel clipped to its unstable reel-seat was the same cheap and noisy bait-casting job that I'd inherited along with my father's steel pole. Once at the river mouth on a blue and white day of soaring seagulls and brisk breeze I stood belly deep in brackish water, doing my best to drive one of the snelled flies from the auction creel into the teeth of the wind.

The fly made a sloppy landing. I let the current take it. At the limit of its swing, all hell broke loose. A swirl big around as a washtub erupted out there where the wavelets danced. A violent, sustained pull all but wrenched the rod from my hands. The reel surrendered line with a squeal of hard-used metal. Its spool held only seventy-five feet of peeling enamelled line, the last of which flashed through the guides of a rod bent almost double. Followed a jar and a harp-string twang. The line had snapped where it was secured to the reel spindle. As for my reel, its handle refused to turn. Under the fierce strain of an assault from what I took to be a roving coho salmon, it had disgorged its ancient innards. We were churchmouse poor, subsisting on these river visitations mainly on trout and potatoes. My father might sympathize, but I knew he lacked the funds to help me buy another reel.

There are times, however, when the wind does favour the

shorn lamb. Thinking dark thoughts, I trudged across the flats to shelter on the downwind side of a massive stump deposited at high tide line by a winter gale. Someone had put in there before me. By the ring of blackened charcoal, he had lit a fire. Fisherman, I decided: he'd fallen in and squelched up here to dry his clothes.

Something green at the edge of the charred circle caught my eye. I stooped to pick up a folded wad of wrinkled paper. Money! I unfolded the wad with fingers made clumsy by excitement. A ten-dollar American bill, and clinging to it a larger Canadian five-spot. Here was treasure untold. Here was much more than the price of a new reel.

That afternoon Dad drove us into Courtenay, where in a secondhand store I found a flyreel, a sturdy Pfleuger with an almost new King Eider flyline already spooled on it, priced at four dollars and fifty cents. Out of the surplus of my windfall, I bought six dozen flyhooks as basic materials for a new and absorbing interest that had come into my life, and a sirloin big enough to overlap our frying pan. Most of the rest went for such basics as porridge oats, strawberry jam and pork and beans.

The new interest was fly-tying. One sultry afternoon I was sitting on a freshet-deposited log by Willows pool, struggling to tie a segment of gull feather to a hook with yarn unravelled from a sock, when a shadow fell across me. Dick James, the big Welshman with the two-handed greenheart rod, stood behind me.

"Well, then," Dick said in his lilting voice. "Is it a fly you'll be making?"

He leaned closer to look.

"Ach!" he snorted in disgust. "That's not the way of it at all."

He lowered himself to the log. From a creel even larger and more battered than our auction basket, he took a tin box that had once held a hundred Players Navy Cut cigarettes. He chose a small pair of scissors from the box, also a darning needle set in a wooden handle, and a spool of black thread. Then he reached for my aborted fly, stripped the gull feather off it, and with deliberately slow movements of his large, mine-scarred fingers, proceeded through the stages of constructing a Plain Coachman.

Fascinated, I watched him nip a pinch of golden pheasant neck feather fibres for a tail. This he secured to the hook with a turn of his silk thread and a half hitch. Then he plucked several strands of iridescent green herl from a peacock tail segment, and wound them on the hook. Like magic, a fat juicy-bug body materialized under his fingers. At the top of the body, he then tied in the butt of a brown neck feather from a rooster — hackle, he called it — which he wound on to form a prickling ruff. This he tweaked and stroked and snipped until it formed a beard under the throat of a fly that now lacked only wings. These Dick scissored from two paired white duck pinions. He held them nipped together in the pincers of his callused thumb and forefinger while he mounted them at the head of his fly with several turns of thread and another half hitch.

Fingers moving almost too fast for my eyes to follow, Dick neated the fly head with a whip finish, then nipped off the tag of thread remaining. He completed his Coachman with a dab of varnish applied to its head with the point of his darning needle dipped into a tiny bottle from his kit. What he had made, explaining each move as he proceeded, was an elegant trout fly.

"Now, then," he commanded. "Let's see you tie one."

Under his coaching, with many a fumble and considerable waste of material, I concocted a fly of sorts. When it was time for the wings, Dick checked me.

"We'll make this a hair wing," he told me. "At times there's nothing will beat a hair wing."

The white hair came from the underside of a deer tail which Dick pulled from one of his jacket side pockets. The hair was slippery stuff. It defied my first attempts to tie it in place, slipping under the fly's belly. But after Dick had drilled me in the pincer-like hold that kept the hair in place, I finally succeeded.

Dick inspected the fly—my firstborn—critically.

"Ah, well," he said. "Perhaps there's a trout stupid enough to take it."

He restored his field kit to his creel, gave me a friendly bunt in the shoulder and clumped on upstream, a rough-hewn friend and one of the many to whom I owe so much for instruction and example in my river years.

One thing about fly-tying I promptly learned: a fly-tier's existence is enlivened by a constant search for materials. Fur and feather, tinsel and hair and silk, all are grist for his busy mill. I had hooks. I had wool from which to spin fly bodies, and already I had designs on the sheaf of peacock tail feathers my mother kept in a vase in our home parlour.

My father once—and only once—tried to help me by obtaining a handful of colourful parrot feathers. We were strolling through one of Vancouver's Hastings Park exhibition buildings when Dad spied a large and highly ornate bird in a tall wire cage. The parrot had neck feathers of a striking iridescent green.

"Think you could use a couple of those?" Dad asked, with a nod at the parrot, which sat scratching its head with one claw while it regarded us from obsidian eyes.

Without waiting for a reply, Dad advanced on the cage. He slipped a hand between the bars and made a quick snatch for those gaudy neck feathers. But the parrot was quicker still. All in a flash, it swivelled its head and clamped its scimitar beak on Dad's finger.

Dad tried to snatch his hand away. The parrot flapped its wings and teetered on its perch, but kept its grip. An attendant hurried up. He opened the cage door, gathered up the parrot with one expert hand, and produced sunflower seed from his pocket with the other. The parrot, preferring seeds to human flesh, opened its beak.

"You mustn't try to pet the birds," the attendant told my father severely.

I lost out on the parrot feathers. What I also lacked was hackle, the glossy ruff from a rooster's neck that was an essential part of a trout fly.

I schemed. I put my wits to work. On the farm we skirted on our way to the Oyster estuary were chickens in plenty.

"Dad," I suggested, "if we had a chicken for Sunday, could you cook it?"

My father gave me a surprised glance. As an old soldier, he had learned by necessity to be a competent plain cook. He could take a can of corned beef, crumble a round or two of pilot bread into it, add onion and pepper, salt and a dash of canned cow, and whip up a hash that was a treat to the taste buds.

Now he gave me a dry answer. "I think I might just manage."

"I'll buy the chicken," I said. After all, I still had several dollars left from my beach find.

The farmer was off with his tractor when I put in at his place. His wife answered when I tapped on the back door. Why, yes, she'd be glad to let us have a chicken. From behind the kitchen door, she took a .22 calibre Winchester pump action rifle which she set in my hands.

"Those birds are wild as grouse," she said. "Only way you'll get one is to shoot its head off."

Her voice followed me as I headed out to the barnyard. "You be careful with that gun—it's loaded!"

Rifle across my knees, I sat on the edge of a watering trough and sized up the fowl that clucked and pecked in a corner of the yard. Most of them were squatty hens, Plymouth Rocks and Buff Orpingtons. Hens were no use to me. What I must have was a well-hackled rooster. Then I spotted him, lord of the harem, strutting on the edge of his busy flock.

He was a tall old Buff, arrogant in his pride, with a shiny

brown neckpiece that caused my hands to tighten on the gun. I set the Winchester to my shoulder, pumped a cartridge into the chamber, and drew a bead on the rooster. Not on his head, though. I didn't want those splendid hackles to be messed up.

At the crack of the rifle, he dropped flopping in a cloud of dust. Jubilant, I gathered him in and returned the gun to the farm wife, who looked at my bird in dismay.

"Oh, dear!" she cried. "You've gone and shot Old Billy. And right through the meat, too!"

I lugged my prize home. Dad frowned over it where it lay claws up on our crude camp table.

"This fellow's going to be tough eating," he said. "It didn't help that you shot him through the gizzard, either." Little I cared! Old Billy had provided me with glossy hackles enough to last me for years. Next on my list of needfuls came deer hair. I knew where to find that. At the first upstream bend, well within sight of the highway bridge, a logjam angled its way half across the river. Near the head of the jam where the entrance riffle galloped in I had spotted the carcass of a blacktail doe tumbled down by a spring freshet to lodge among the tangle of debris.

Next morning, I ventured up that way alone, pausing to swim a fly through likely pools and runs. When I came to the logjam, I cached my rod in a willow thicket and teetered out along one of the key logs that wedged the jam in place. The defunct doe announced her presence with a miasmic stench. But I wanted her scut badly. Holding my breath, I edged out toward where she lay with rump cocked in air. Jackknife open in my hand, I knelt on the log, made a long reach, and grabbed her tail. A couple of slashes and it came free. I rammed it into one pocket, closed my knife and dropped it in my other pocket, then rocked to my feet in triumph.

But that triumph was shortlived. As I edged around on the timber stick to make for the bank, a loose shard of bark skidded under my left foot. I staggered, fought with wildly waving arms to regain my balance, then plummeted through an interstice between logs into the river.

The current snatched me and hustled me along. Just short of the instant when I would be sucked under the jam to share the blacktail doe's fate, I got an arm across a low-trailing sweeper. There I hung, legs trailing in the fierce current with black depth under me.

No use to yell for my father. He was a quarter-mile away in camp. If I were to escape from this trap, it must be by my own efforts.

I got my other arm over the sweeper. Inch by inch, with an effort that strained every muscle, I hauled myself along it.

The current released its grip. My legs were out of water. A log crossed my sweeper. I transferred to that one, squirrelled along it, and poked my head through a litter of withered boughs and wood fragments into blessed sunlight.

Safe off the jam, shaky-legged and sober, I retrieved my rod and limped off along the bar toward camp.

I had come within an ace of paying the ultimate price for that crop of bucktail. The episode taught me a lesson. A river has two faces. One is fair to the eye, all sunshine and sparkle, shadow and light in enchanting variety. The other is the face of death. I loved my river still, but I had learned to respect her. Through the years she has drowned more than one swimmer or fisherman who failed to do so. That evening, at the tail of the bridge pool, I hooked my first trout on a fly of my own tying. Since then I have tied hundreds, I suppose thousands, of trout flies. The list takes in sinking wet flies and high-floating dry flies. Grey Wulffs and Brown Bivisibles, Peter Rosses and American Coachmen and that paragon which would be my choice were I confined to a single enticement, the red-and-yellow hairwing Mickey Finn.

As a thank you to Dick James, that master tier, I have passed the knack on to others. Some were boys, some were bedridden men and women. A few were pensioners eager to learn a craft with which they might augment their slender incomes.

Once I even assisted my friend Ted Davis, skilled Victoria tier, at a night school class in the art. It went very well, although we did have to run a couple of our more impetuous students to hospital emergency for the removal of hooks embedded in fingers or thumbs.

I should add that my father transmuted Old Billy into a Sunday stew fortified with carrots and onions, potatoes and slices of Swede turnip. It was delectable, and only a trifle tough.

6.

Upriver

THERE WERE PROFOUND DIFFERENCES between Will Mayse on our river and the Reverend Amos W. Mayse in his pulpit at Nanaimo's First Baptist Church. The one looked as if he had crept out of a hole in the bank. His ratty old pants were patched on the seat. If it happened to be raining, he wore a tattered yellow oilskin coat over his work shirt. A mushroom-shaped hat with drooping brim topped this ensemble.

The Reverend Mr. Mayse presented a different picture. His black boots twinkled from the elbow grease I expended on them each Saturday night. His high collar was stiffly starched, his trousers creased to a knife edge, and his black broadcloth cutaway coat—which he called a Prince Albert—lent the final touch of dignity.

Nor was the change merely a matter of appearance. On the river we were comrades, equal in our desire to catch the biggest possible trout. In town we reverted to the standard father-and-son relationship. I had chores to do: my mother's woodbox to be kept filled, grass to cut, chickens to feed and their shed to clean.

Also, while Sunday might be a day of rest for the privileged, it was not so for me. I had the inner workings of the church to keep me busy. These consisted of lighting and stoking the furnace in winter, sweeping the mouse-coloured carpet runners in the aisles and, if it happened to be Communion Sunday, filling the wine glasses and ranging them on their tray.

Not that my father's straitlaced congregation would tolerate the use of honest-to-goodness alcoholic wine. What they wanted and what I poured for them was Welch's grape juice, with a surreptitious nip or two for me on the side.

Another task when the new converts were to come up for baptism was to run cold water into the zinc-lined, waist-deep baptistry to the left of the pulpit, and bring it to a seemly temperature. This last was accomplished by lighting a fire in the standup water heater in the church basement. Beside the heater was a pile of coal, delivered in chunks the size of ice blocks, which I was required to break up with the back of an axe. I then kindled a cedar blaze in the heater, added wood slabs and, when these were well alight, shovelled in the coal.

I was then free for a couple of hours. A while before morning service I would test the heat of the water with a bare foot. If it was warm enough, I would go down to the basement and close the heater drafts as well as the valve that fed hot water from tank to baptistry.

One ill-starred Sabbath morning with a baptism on the books, I hurried through my usual drill. Lit the fire, stoked the heater generously with coal, opened all drafts, then took myself off to enjoy the hour or so remaining before service. It was horse chestnut time. I became involved in a game of cobbers—jousting with horse chestnuts tied to a string—and scurried guiltily to my stool beside the organ as the congregation rose for the first hymn.

The service dragged on. Finally, while the collection was being taken, my father retired from his pulpit to the anteroom at the back of the church. When he reappeared, his feet were cased in the chunky rubber boots attached to his waders—not his yellow trout-chasers this time, but his formal black baptizing pair.

Craning around from my job of pumping the organ, I watched my father lead the male convert to the baptistry steps.

My father descended first. As the water rose around his knees, he shot me one awful glance.

In absolute horror, I realized what I'd done. The water was gently steaming: I'd forgotten to damp down the drafts and close the valve.

But my father was equal to the occasion. He reached for the white-gowned convert, landed him in the baptistry with a single jerk of a powerful arm, clapped a hand over mouth and nose to stifle his cries, dunked him and raised him in one swift motion. Then he propelled him, lobster red and steaming, up the steps. My father, also steaming, followed with iron dignity. The service proceeded.

Walking home with my mother, sister and father, I waited nervously for the sky to fall. But my father did not acknowledge my sin of omission by word or deed until we turned in at our gate. He motioned me to enter ahead of him. As I sidled past, he fetched me a roundhouse skelp on my behind that skittered me a dozen feet along the front walk.

"What were you trying to do?" he demanded. "Boil me alive?"

Through all the rubs and scrapes and disappointments of a small town preacher's life, my father preserved a faith that never wavered. Most of his ironbound congregation would have preferred sermons that dwelt on hellfire and damnation rather than love and forgiveness. But my father had no more truck than need be with a vengeful Jehovah. He was a New Testament man, and his sermons were never better than when he drew his inspiration from one or other of the apostles.

His favourite Easter Sunday sermon was based on that marvellous passage in the Gospel according to Saint John, where the fishermen disciples find the risen Christ on the lakeside by a fire of coals "and fish laid thereon, and bread."

As he dealt with that resurrection story, my father would stand taller. His voice would deepen with emotion: his face would glow.

I never loved my father more than in those moments. Perhaps some of his congregation were moved by his earnestness, but most sat wooden-faced and untouched.

Eventually, this majority element persuaded the church authority to send them another pastor. We removed to Vancouver and a little East End church where my father continued to serve his God faithfully and without complaint. He was a simple man and a good one, the best I've known.

As for me, I hated Vancouver cordially, and lived for the day when I could get back to Vancouver Island. August came. On its first day, my father began to load our stained old wall tent and other camping gear into our car.

He gave me his leather-faced grin. "Well," he said, "how about lending a hand?"

"Where are we going?" I asked him, hardly daring to hope.

"To Oyster River," he told me. "If we hustle, we can catch the ten o'clock ferry."

That summer, my fifteenth, was memorable. For one thing, at long last, my father and I pulled off a proper upriver expedition.

Fishermen's rumours of the "long as your arm" persuasion are a dime a dozen. One of these had come to my father's ever-receptive ears.

"You know," he said to me, "I've heard there's a run of big trout goes up the Oyster right about now. They travel fast, at night. We never see them." He paused for effect, then continued. "If you're lucky enough to hit those trout up there, you get fishing you wouldn't believe." He concluded solemnly, "Bill, those trout are as long as your arm!"

For trout that size, I could brave even the rumoured wild bulls of the upriver fastnesses. We set out next morning in the first grey light of dawn. The night before, Dad had produced a large-scale forestry map of the upriver area, and we had pored over it by candlelight on our whacked-together camp table.

"We won't try to go with the river," Dad said. "Too tough. What we'll do is follow this old logging grade here" — his finger traced the route — "to the butt of this sidehill here, then we'll cut across country." His finger jabbed again. "That should bring us to the river about here."

"What'll we do if we run into Two-Ton Tony?" I asked. Two-Ton Tony was a wild bull made legendary by his cunning, his size and his unparalleled ferocity.

"Climb a stump," my father said, "and pray."

So in the morning's earliest light we crossed the highway bridge and followed a dirt road that headed back toward the mountains. All was shadowy and indistinct. Down-logs by the roadside became prowling cougars. Charred stumps of the old burn were bears rampant, waiting to rush upon us. I stuck close to Dad's jacket tails with more than one nervous backward glance, and when a late-faring horned owl loosed its chesty hoot, I all but jumped out of my skin.

By the time the sky lightened, we had turned off the road

onto an old logging right-of-way that ambled inland at a tangent to our original course. Its railway steel had long since been taken up and its hemlock sleepers had mostly rotted away. Tag alder crowded waist-high along it, and tall Scotch thistles bordered its winding course.

Time passed. The sun rose all glorious at our backs, gaining warmth with altitude. Too soon we were sweltering in the dry inland heat of the burn. This was desolate country, ravaged by man and then left to nature's slow healing and to the wild things that returned to it when the loggers had moved on. A hawk hung as if suspended by its wingtips in a milky sky that deepened to bronze at its horizons. The whalebacked ridge for which we were heading grew no closer.

My father, veteran of many a forced march, seemed tireless. He trudged on, creel riding his hip, cased rod aswing in one hand. I longed for him to call a halt, but this he didn't do until another hour had passed. We came to a lost little thread of a creek that whispered in a stony channel. Here at last Dad halted.

"We'll take ten," he said. He regarded me with a glint of humour in his brown eyes. "Try soaking your feet in the creek," he suggested. "That helps."

I peeled runners and holed socks from my hot and aching feet, and dangled them in a miniature basin among the creek stones. The water was cool, its touch welcome. While I hunched there, Dad opened his creel. He brought out two bottles of root beer and two chocolate bars.

We ate and we drank. We plodded on. At long last the sidehill moved in on us, approaching steadily until we halted in its shadow. Dad consulted his map again.

"Fine," he said. "So far, so good. Now, if we cut across here" — his finger tapped and traced — "we should hit the river just about where the fellow said those big trout lie up." He pocketed his map and regarded me in high good humour. "This way, we save ourselves a few miles of foot-slogging."

So we tramped on across the desert of stumps where sprawling wild blackberry vines snatched at our feet. In the occasional deep-burned pocket where the slash fires had left a layer of fine charcoal, black dust rose in choking, blinding clouds around us. Twice we spotted little bands of wild cattle—wild in the sense that MacIvor and others turned them loose in the burns to forage year-round, culling a few for slaughter each fall—and my throat went dry at the sight of them. But we saw no bulls among the scattered cows, and as soon as they winded us, they drifted off into the farther distance. They were the true Cattle of the Sun, many of them calved in the wild, fiercely horned, shy of humans and fleet as deer.

More hours passed. The river failed to materialize. Finally Dad drew out his map and stood spraddle-legged, frowning down at it.

"We're away off the track," he said. He took a battered nickel-cased compass from his pocket, set it on a low stump, and bent over it. Then he straightened and pointed. Far to the northwest, a dimly seen green line wavered across the edge of our world.

"There's our river," he said. "Those are the alders along it."

At that point, while my heart was in my shoes and the journey across the flat to those faraway trees seemed quite impossible, my father came up with one of those gestures that made him a man apart. From his creel he took his bottle of root beer, still half full and with the top smacked into place. Another grope brought out half his chocolate bar, neatly folded into its wrapper. He handed me bottle and bar.

"We'll take another break," he said, "then have at it."

Evening was close when we pulled in to our strayed river. Its murmur swelled louder through the flanking alders. Then there it was: up here a swifter, narrower stream that dropped through a frothing cascade into a long rock-walled basin.

"This looks like the place," Dad said, "but we're too beat

to fish it this evening." He squinted up at the declining sun, which now slanted low into the west. "We'll rustle some wood and make a fire," he said. "Then we'll settle in and be comfortable."

"But we have to get back to camp," I protested. "We can't stay here all night!"

My father gave me a look of complete surprise. "Why not?" he asked. "Weather's mild. It won't rain. You'll enjoy it."

To my amazement, I did. Dad's creel yielded a tin of the corned beef by which he set such store. We ate it cold in fat-marbled chunks with rounds of pilot bread, a spartan meal washed down with river water. Then we built up our fire and settled our shoulders against a log. I did not expect to sleep, but I hadn't reckoned on the effect of a day's bushwhacking.

The fire conversed softly with itself. Overhead flowed the Milky Way, a river of stars. The last thing I saw was my father's broad and weathered face. Firelight turned his forehead ruddy. His lower face was shadowed except where a red glow told of the pipe clamped between his teeth.

I woke to birdsong and dew that diamonded the pink-purple fireweed. The sun was well up. Dad squatted by the ring of river stones within which we'd laid our fire. He was lighting another blaze. Beside him on a log end were the half-full tin of corned beef and a couple more pilot bread rounds.

We ate. Dad burned out and buried the bully beef tin. Then we set up our rods and crossed the bleached white freshet bar to the river. A sand patch held the round pussycat tracks of a cougar. From the wooded opposite bank, a blacktail doe watched us. We waded the riffle that tumbled into the rocky basin. The strong water pushed hard at our legs. Arms locked for support, we crabbed our way across the impetuous current.

Dad threaded a worm on his hook. I tied on a Royal Coachman, one of the flies made in hope during the winter. I crunched on down toward the tail of the pool, leaving Dad to work his spinner through the middle deep.

As my eyes grew accustomed to the bewildering dance and play of surface currents I saw, lying close to the bottom a few feet from where the river spilled into its exit rapid, several long grey shadows that hung stationary over golden gravel. Then a current-flaw opened a window in the flow. Through water clear as air, I saw those shadows take form and substance.

Trout! And not merely trout. These were the biggest cutthroat I had ever seen in my life. We had found the August run. I waded deeper into the shallows and began to work out line. The fly dropped well upstream of the cutthroat squadron, giving it time to sink before it flirted past their predacious noses. As it passed, one of those king-sized trout exposed its white jaw-lining in what looked uncommonly like a yawn.

For an hour we worked the basin, Dad with his usually potent spinner and worm combination, me with a variety of flies. The net result of our labours was a seven-inch tiddler that charged my Mickey Finn. Hauled out on the bar, rods resting against our knees, we took counsel.

"Maybe they don't feed when they're up here," I suggested gloomily.

"Or maybe we're just not giving them what they want," Dad said.

He turned to his creel and woodchucked his way into its depths to come up with a dogeared envelope. From the envelope, he shook half a dozen monstrous flies on to his palm. They were bass flies, three times the size of my confections—garish affairs fat-bodied and heavily hackled, tied in a variety of brilliant colours. We had regarded them more as curiosities than as lures to be actually fished with. Now I watched in surprise while Dad snipped his spinner free and knotted one of those outsized flies to his leader.

"You don't think that'll work?" I said in complete scepticism.

"Maybe not," Dad said, dangling the enormous red-and-white Parmachene Belle. "But it could shock them into hitting."

He nipped a couple of split shot weights to his leader with his teeth, then waded into the stream with the big fly dancing like a hummingbird at the end of his leader. Anchored knee deep, he pulled line off the Uniqua and lobbed out a cast. His offering landed with a splash; the current took it. Paying out more line, Dad let the split shot bounce his lure the length of the basin. Or almost the full length. Down where I'd seen the great cutties ranged in soldierly rows, a sudden eruption sent a boil to the surface. An instant later, Dad loosed his Fish on! yell, and leaned back hard on his bucking rod.

We did not carry landing nets, preferring to skid our played-out fish up the pebbles. But when I saw the size of Dad's trout, now finning weakly in a few inches of water, I wished most fervently for a net.

"Get in behind him," Dad ordered. "If he comes unpinned, don't let him past you!"

He backed, rod straining, up the stony slope. When it felt shingle beneath its belly, the trout panicked in a splurge that half-blinded me with flying spray. Then, as Dad slid it clear, I got both hands behind it and scooped it up past the point of escape.

For a long moment, we stared at it in awe.

"Long as your arm," Dad said, and I answered him, "Darn near."

Perfectly conditioned, glowing in gold and silver and spotted like the pard, it lay long and broad-sided at our feet. It was so recently up from the Strait that parasitic sea lice still clustered at its vent.

"It'll go four pounds," Dad said. "Close to five."

He spread his jacket over his prize to keep it from the sun.

The next and last trout came to a huge Grizzly King that I tied on with trembling fingers. It was of a size with my father's fish: they made a noble pair. By this time the sun was blazing down, and those long grey shadows were no longer on station above the pool-tail gravel. They had sought shelter among the massive boulders that studded the basin. But we were more than content. We had intercepted the fabled midsummer run of whoppers and taken tribute.

Since one of those big cutthroat was all we could handle, I made a gift of the other to the farmer's wife. She thanked me for it, stuffed me with gingersnaps fresh from her oven, and invited me to another chicken.

7.

The Golden Gates

ONE OF THE CROSSES that my father had to bear as a small-church pastor was the occasional descent upon his town of some hot gospeleering evangelist. These exotic birds of passage arrived with considerable fanfare. A few set up circus-type tents for their revivals. Most rented a hall or the local arena. They drew large crowds, including congregation members from all sects, whom they whipped to a state bordering on hysteria by their often eloquent exhortations. They paid lip service to the love of God and the forgiveness of sins, but leaned far more heavily on the fear of hellfire. At the close of one of their productions the aisles would be choked with repentant sinners, many in tears, coming forward to claim conversion.

Some of the evangelists dealt in faith healing and produced, as in the case of one of my father's hardnosed and wilful flock, startling if evanescent results.

Old Charlie Ransom had been a two-crutch cripple for many years. From my observation post at the back of the hall, I saw him join the pathetic file of halt and lame advancing at the close of a revival whoop-up for a laying-on of hands.

Charlie's turn came. The evangelist put his hands on Charlie's shoulders. He raised his bland white face heavenward and uttered a loud and sonorous prayer: "Oh Lord, look on this afflicted brother, thy servant. Take pity on his infirmity and make him whole!"

He straightened. So did Charlie, who gave his head a shake as if dazed, then dropped his crutches and walked out of the hall praising the Almighty at every step. To all appearances he was a miraculously recovered man.

Power of faith? Applied psychology? A form of mesmerism? We can only guess. In any case, Charlie's recovery was short-lived. Next Sunday morning, the evangelist off to new fields, Charlie turned up late and still crutchless for service. Midway to his pew, he halted and stood swaying while the sweat beaded on his forehead and his lips mumbled incoherent words. Then he fell heavily, to huddle weeping on the floor. It remained for my father to talk Charlie out of suicide. He never walked without crutches again.

That was the dark side of the evangelists' moon. Simple men and women choused into religious fervour tumbled back all too soon into the gritty, grimy monotony of their everyday lives. Disillusioned, some gave up the church. Others lingered, taking out their discontent on the minister, who was required to pick up the pieces. Another negative result of these visits was that they mopped up money which normally would have gone into a congregation's collection envelopes. This speedily worsened the pastor's already tight-strained economy.

In fairness, not all the evangelists were money-grubbing charlatans. The one I remember best was Gypsy Smith—the name under which he delivered his message—a swarthy, handsome man with long, coal-black hair and flashing black eyes. He was true Romany. As a youth he had roved with a gypsy caravan in England, living a wild, untrammelled and interestingly sinful life until a light broke on him and he turned to religion. He was a fine eloquent man, never one to deal in scare tactics or to induce euphoria, and the fact that my father liked and respected him was enough for me.

One Sunday afternoon between services, I coaxed Gypsy Smith into going for a walk by the Millstream. He paced with a light and soundless tread along the tree-bordered path, with eyes that saw more of nature's ways than I could ever hope to see. The trail was interrupted by a rock ledge above the stream. Gypsy Smith knelt and studied the gliding water intently for a moment. Then he shed his jacket, rolled his shirt sleeve to the shoulder, and inch by inch, lowered his hand into the run. He sprawled on the ledge for what seemed to me a long time. Then he withdrew his dripping arm. Clutched in his brown hand was a lively eleven-inch trout.

"Are you going to keep it?" I asked, scarce able to believe the evidence of my eyes.

Gypsy Smith's gold earrings flashed as he shook his head.

"No need," he said. "Let it keep the life God gave it."

He opened his hand, and the "tickled" trout returned to its element.

There were other evangelists. Billy Sunday, short, sweaty and energetic, sprinkled his exhortations with baseball metaphors culled from his days as a professional player. Aime Semple Macpherson, a statuesque redhead in a white robe, knew the uses of melodrama and attracted vast crowds to her carefully staged extravaganzas. They came and they went, leaving my father and other run-of-the-mill ministers to mend the fences and tidy up after them.

By this time in my life I knew what I wanted to be, thanks in large part to an enlightened woman by the name of Grace Luckhart who was features editor of the Vancouver *Daily Province*. She printed some of the squibs I sent her, and even saw that I got paid for them, a dispensation that kept me clothed and left me a dollar or two for the always lean family kitty. So a writer I would be, and I celebrated the fact at the age of twelve by turning out a short story which was accepted by *Canadian Magazine*. The editor kept my story for two mortal years unpaid-for, then his magazine turned up its toes. At least he had the grace to send my story back.

I laboriously retyped it on my father's Oliver and sent it off to the *Toronto Star Weekly*, a journal which in its day did much to encourage young writers. Glory be! The *Star* not only accepted, but sent me a cheque for a princely thirty-five dollars.

Next day I played hookey from Vancouver's Britannia High School, where I was an indifferent student. I bought a hamburger and a bottle of Hires root beer and took myself off to a stretch of vacant land above Burrard Inlet. There I lay in the long grass, watching white puffball clouds sail across the blue, and dreaming large dreams. The golden gates had opened. I was on my way. Life mercifully allows us no perspective on the future. I had no way of knowing that my next eighty-five stories would go unbought. Happier than I had ever been in my life, I planned how I would spend my fortune. I'd buy a really good flyrod, perhaps even an English Hardy, than which there was no better.

After due deliberation I bought a Hardy Kohinor, a five-ounce aristocrat designed for tournament work. Its eight-foot-nine of powerful and marvellously balanced two-piece split cane could be depended upon to drive a fly out against any wind short of a gale. I have that Kohinor still. In fact, it remains top rod in my considerable battery. In spite of age and hard use—sometimes brutally hard—it remains straight and resilient. No year goes by that I don't take a trout or two on it.

Time passed. The *Star* printed my story. A few days later, I was summoned to the principal's office. He had a copy of the *Toronto Star Weekly* on his desk, and a frown on his meaty face.

We had never seen eye to eye. An unreconstructed Englishman, the principal was a fanatical devotee of cricket, a game for which I had no liking whatever. I had also headed up a revolt against school cadets and won a partial victory in that a squad of like-minded boys and I were allowed to form a signal corps. The Canadian Department of National Defence paid us five dollars each and gave us certificates when we completed our course. On cadet parade days, we signallers split our ranks and withdrew to opposite ends of the school ground, where we wigwagged dirty messages to each other in the knowledge that only the elect could get the drift of them.

The principal tapped my *Star* story with a finger. This sort of thing, he told me, must stop. I was trying to run before I had learned to walk. In future I would pay attention to my English teachers, absorbing what they in their wisdom could teach me, and not be so presumptuous as to rush into publication. He then dropped a not-too-subtle hint that if I failed to heed his ukase, I might find myself expelled. After a further homily on the virtues of discipline and my need for the same, His Nibs dismissed me.

I was mad as a hornet. The injustice, the sheer fatheadedness, of his remarks stung me to the quick. When I told my father about the principal's edict, he showed no visible reaction until I had finished my tale of woe. Then he said mildly, "I think I'd better go have a talk with that man."

This he did. Neither he nor the principal told me how their conversation proceeded. But next day I got a curt note from the principal's secretary informing me that if I insisted on writing for publication the school would not interfere.

The term ended. I scraped through with a grudging pass. August came, and with it release from city bondage. My father and I headed for our river, me with my new Kohinor in my gear.

Our first day at the estuary was windy. Waves slopped over my hip-boot tops as I took up station well out from the entrance bar. A few yards away, my father's sturdy figure bulked reassuringly. Life was very good.

On a day like this, with water roiled and wind-patterned, a large fly would serve better than a small one. I chose a size six Teal and Silver from the box that held the serried ranks of a winter's fly-tying, and knotted it to my leader tippet.

The Kohinor, gutsy yet limber, was a treat to handle. I

punched the big Teal and Silver into the wind, rejoicing in the way my flyline sailed out in a flat arc. Several casts later, I felt a gentle tap-tap at my fly. I cocked my rod wrist, felt the hook engage, and knew at once that what I had at the end of my leader was no trout. It had a weight and an authority that told the story. Salmon!

Fortune favoured me as I played the salmon. My big, scarred Pfleuger reel held a ninety-foot flyline and fifty yards of linen backing. Also, the fish chose to stay within the channel bounded by the kelp beds and bars that stretched north away from the river mouth. Even so, there were times when it bowed the Kohinor like a willow in a wind, and had my hard-pressed reel down to its last couple of feet of backing.

I worked on the fish until my rod arm ached from weariness and my shirt was sweat-plastered to my back. At long last, the salmon went with the pull of the line, letting me lead him into a cove between stony points. The fish, I could tell from his broad black-spotted olive back, was of heart-stopping size. As his belly touched the shingle, he surged and flounced mightily. But my father had worked his way behind him, and now stooped to secure him with a two-handed grab behind his flaring gill covers.

Dad carried my fish flapping up the beach, to knock him on the head and lay him in the shade of a drift log. We stood looking down at His Majesty where he lay in silver-bronze and patterned green splendour. A Chinook salmon. Later in camp, he weighed in at eighteen pounds. For a flyrod, no mean trophy!

For days afterward my arm ached. But the Kohinor had come through the battle entirely un-damaged. It had done the rodmakers of Merry England proud.

8.
A Miracle of Fishes

ONE MORNING IN CAMP my desire to create a wonder-fly that no trout could resist lured me into grievous error. I raided my father's prized shaving brush for a tuft of its two-toned badger bristles.

Shaving day came — when we were at the river, Dad relaxed his daily shaving routine, turning to his old-fashioned straight-edge only twice a week — and Dad emerged from our tent with brush in hand and a face like thunder.

"My brush," he accused. "You've ruined it."

Caught cold, I could offer no plea. Dad gave me a look that would fry an egg, then with no other word spoken, took his rod from where it leaned rigged and ready against a tree, shouldered his creel, and marched off toward the upriver trail.

Guilty and disconsolate, I mooched around camp. Time dragged. I undertook to construct my fly, which when completed turned out to be not such-a-much. Lunchtime came, but for once I didn't feel like eating. The afternoon stretched endless. I lugged water from the ravine spring and split a reserve pile of wood. Evening approached, and still no trace of my father.

The mustard seed of worry I'd been entertaining swelled to pumpkin size when dinnertime came and passed, and still no Dad. It was a harsh and lonely country, the upriver. A man could have an accident up there, come to grief and none the wiser. Also, there were those bulls.

With the sun close to setting and the shadows lengthening, I could wait no longer. I set our dinner, the dinner I'd prepared as food of repentance, on the back of our camp stove and set out to find my strayed father.

If he were heading for camp, it might well be along the old logging grades that spread their network on either side of the river. Hurrying, trotting where the going was good, I headed in from the highway. I came to the first of the sidehills that shouldered down to the stream without sight or sound of Dad. Heart sinking, I hustled on. I'd been sure we would cross trails on the stretch of old logging railway I'd covered.

Another mile, with the twilight deepening, and still no sign of him. A dim and tangled grade branched off the main line I had been following. I knew that it led down to one of Dad's favourite upriver pools, a long, deep and narrow run confined between a freshet bar and a clay cutbank. I started into the old grade. It was almost dark in there, and eerie, with alders crowding in on the right-of-way from either side.

Something moved in the dimness ahead.

"Dad?" I called in a voice that wobbled in spite of me.

But it was not my father. Something darker than the dusk reared up off the grade a scant ten feet in front of me. Neck prickling, mouth agape, I froze in my tracks. This was the stuff of nightmare: the thing looked big as a house. With a startled *Woof!* the creature dropped to all fours and racketed into the alder cover with a crackling of brush. A bear. A black bear, up on its hind legs to look me over before it took off, at least as terrified as I was.

Still icy cold between my shoulders, I groped my way on down the grade. The river voice swelled loud in my ears. I'd put all my chips on finding Dad at that pool, feasting perhaps, or enjoying an extra-good bout of late fishing. But the bar with its skull-sized white stones glimmered empty. I could go on upriver or trace the stream down over two miles of bar and riffle, pool and treed tongue of land, to the highway bridge and camp. Dad would most surely be on his way to camp by now. I elected to follow the ribbon of lighter sky downstream.

As I progressed, I tried to comfort myself by remembering that my father was at home in the outdoors as a fish in water. He was never happier than when off in wild country, a heritage that he had passed on to me and to other boys who came within his influence.

One of Dad's hopes at his Nanaimo pastorate had been to organize a Boy Scout troop and a Wolf Cub pack. But his deacons—always those infernal, downbeat deacons!—had vetoed the suggestion. The Boy Scouts wore uniforms, did they not? And were they not a militaristic organization subject to quasi-military discipline?

My father did his best to allay their fusty doubts and fears. The Scout and Cub uniforms, he pointed out, were simply sensible wear for outdoor-oriented boys. As for being militaristic, any similarity to the army was surface only, designed to facilitate group effort and to bring out qualities of leadership.

He argued in vain. The deacons had laid their ears back, and were not to be moved by reason. No Scouts. No Cubs.

My father was not one to give in easily. He ferreted out a boys' organization that rejoiced in the name of the Tuxis Rangers. These wore no uniforms, and their name was a play on an internationally recognized peacekeeping establishment, the Texas Rangers. The deacons bought that, though dubiously, and the sons of churchgoers were bullied and dragooned into becoming Tuxis Rangers. As the minister's son I was expected, naturally, to join.

Unfortunately, nobody knew quite what the objects and ideals of the Tuxis Rangers might be. Left in the dark, we muddled along as best as we could. Wednesday nights, we met in the church basement, where my father put us through muscle-building exercises, taught us knot tying, basic woodcraft and first aid and—greatly daring—set up a boxing ring.

From Lord knows where, he scrounged a set of boxing gloves, frayed and old as the hills. These were practice gloves, heavily padded, but the cheap wadding had worked its way off the knuckles so that the blow which landed did so with considerable authority. Even so, we enjoyed boxing, and each Wednesday evening mounted half a dozen bouts enlivened by such encouragements as "Hit 'im in the gut!" or "Kill him!" or "Bust his nose!"

One evening I found myself paired off with a ginger-haired boy fresh out from Scotland. His name was James McGuigan, and he was the son of stiff and godly parents. I liked Jimmy. He was strong as a bull but good-natured, and we got along well. We stepped into the ring. My father laced the gloves on us, enjoined us against low blows, butting and heeling, and turned us loose.

Jimmy started proceedings with the best will in the world by knocking me down. The padding in his glove had slipped: I felt as if I'd been kicked by a mule. To the raucous cheers and jeers of our fellow Tuxis Rangers, I picked myself up and faced Jimmy again.

"I didna' hurt ye, laddie?" he asked anxiously.

"Hell, no!" I muttered. My Nanaimo years had taught me a little about roughhouse battling. I watched my chance, slipped inside Jimmy's guard, if such it could be called, trod on his arch and walloped him in the eye.

That ended the round and the fight. By the time the Tuxis Rangers broke up that night, Jimmy's puffy left eye displayed several interesting shades of purple.

I was both shocked and contrite.

"Gee, Jimmy," I told him, "I'm sorry. I didn't mean to hurt you."

The sunny-tempered Scots boy gave me a grin. "Ah, forget it," he said. "It'll be gey different anither time. Ye arm my fist wi' muckle strength!"

But there was no next time. When Jimmy took his shiner home, his horrified parents complained bitterly to the deacons. As a result, our unit of the Tuxis Rangers, one which never did take wing, was promptly disbanded.

My misplaced father knew his woodcraft and his river. Half a mile downstream, my eyes caught a flicker of light on a bar. Hoping against hope, I floundered through a riffle and hurried on down.

Glory be! It was my dad, right enough, but less than right in his person. He had kindled a little comfort fire. His villainous pipe gave off the occasional waft of smoke. But his left arm was splinted in cedar bark shards lashed on with strips from his hip pocket bandana and belted tight against his side.

"That you, Bill?" He climbed to his feet. "I had a little trouble," he said. "Took a tumble and broke my wrist." He reached his rod from where it leaned against a driftwood root. "Maybe you'll pack the creel," he said.

We bushwhacked our way out to the main logging grade and started down it. Once my father stumbled. Fearing for his self-splinted wrist, I took his other arm, steadying him for a little longer than necessary.

"I'm sorry about that," I muttered. "You know, about your shaving brush."

"Forget it," he said.

That night, walking under a skyful of stars that seemed almost near enough to touch, with the sounds and scents of the burned-over land dark around us, we were very close. That closeness remained through a dinner of congealed fried eggs, cold pork and beans, dry bread to mop up the juices and hell-hot coffee.

Next morning, without benefit of driver's licence, I took

my father in to Courtenay where a doctor set his fractured wrist. That afternoon he was back on the river, slinging a worm and spinner one-handed.

In the night it came on to rain, a gentle patter on the tent canvas at first, then a downpour like the floods of Noah. We rigged a tarp for the protective fly over our cooking fire, stacked our wood in its shelter, then with our axe and a pointed stick, scraped a hasty drainage trench around our camp. We turned in again to the drumming of rain on soaked canvas.

Morning broke late and murky. Dark cloud masses still shunted their way down the river valley from the obscured mountains. Each cloud discharged its cargo of rain on us and our camp. The river raised its voice from a whisper to a sullen growl. It flowed brown and turgid under the highway bridge, and still it rained. That night we burrowed shivering into damp blankets. In the small hours our trench overflowed. When I poked an exploratory hand over the side of my evergreen-filled log crib, it plunged into cold water. All the next day, the rain bucketed down. That night our bedding was not merely damp. It was soaked. With old-soldier fortitude, Dad reminded me that wet wool stays warm, and we crawled in for another miserable night.

On the third morning, the rain tapered off to a drizzle. By mid-afternoon that too had stopped, and there remained only a drip from the trees. Presently off to the westward we saw a narrow band of blue. From that point, clearing was rapid. The sun ventured out. So did we, stiff from prolonged damp, into a steaming world. We had been penned up in our doubtful shelter for most of three mortal days. It was good to be squelching down the river trail toward the Willows pool and the long reach above the estuary.

When we stepped out of the woods at the Willows bend, I thought for a moment that the rain had renewed itself. The long placid reach, tide-swollen, was ringed from one limit to the other with small quiet circles.

"What is it, Dad?" I asked in half a whisper.

"If it is what I think it is," my father said, staring at those myriad rings, "we'd better get down here bright and early tomorrow."

But even he didn't quite realize the extent of what was happening there on a river reach that lay quicksilver in the post-sunset glow. That knowledge burst upon us next morning after a snap-and-swallow breakfast when we waded into the reach, now shrunken by a falling tide.

Trout! Searun cutthroat, fresh in from the saltchuck and hungry as wolves!

I flipped out a fly and was lengthening line for a longer cast when, fifteen feet from my running shoes, the water exploded. My startled yelp was drowned in my father's urgent bellow: "Give me room! I'm into a lunker!"

Dad came splashing and staggering along the shallows, in tow of a fish that had taken the line over its shoulder and was hellbent for the salt water it had so lately quitted. Dad lost that fish. It flung the spinner at the apex of a leap that set me gasping at its size. I skidded my very much smaller searun up the gravel, freed my fly and waded in for more.

The prolonged rains after a two-month dry spell had brought a pirate horde of searun cutties into the lower river. They were wild fish that had never seen a hatchery tank, unsophisticated and hungry. Pugnacious predators, they charged anything and everything we threw at them.

They were typical of their kind — built for dash and speed — with fierce, shapely heads, broad tails and speckled flanks that carried always a subtle underlay of gold. Beautiful to the eye, superlatively good in the pan, they were and remain my favourite fish among the salmonids.

Mystery, never fully solved, obscures their comings and

goings. River-born from eggs spawned on the clean gravel redds, they remain in their home stream for two or three years. Then they descend to the sea as lively smolts. By a dispensation of all-wise nature, the tiny fry of the coho salmon choose the same period in which to make their own descent. The young cutthroat are sustained in their journey by raids on the swarming fry.

What instinct, what inborn yearning impels the juvenile cutthroat to change their venue, one can only guess. I do know that our coastal streams, scouring their way over and through granite, are never rich in bottom feed. In part, it may be this lack that urges them out to the salt where nature offers a more bountiful free lunch. Nor is there any factor in their makeup or in their freshwater life to pick them out from those homebody cutthroat that never go to sea.

Having arrived in tidewater, they feed voraciously upon launce-fish, young herring, shrimp and any other denizen of the inshore waters small enough for them to catch.

For the rest of their lives, they trade in and out of the saltchuck, sometimes foraging in estuaries and the lower courses of streams, often roving the saltwater shorelines for miles as the mood takes them. It used to be generally held that they followed the salmon to their upriver spawning grounds each fall, greedy for dropped eggs that the current rolled down to them. Later and more accurate observations indicate that some of the searun cutthroat, even though their own spawning time is still distant, may loaf their way upstream as early as July, ahead of the salmon. There they remain until late winter or very early spring triggers their own spawning.

This, I should point out, is not a general exodus. I have taken searuns in estuaries and along the beaches when their brothers and gravid sisters are reproducing their kind on nuptial beds a dozen miles inland.

The fact is that even in this era of close investigation and pinpointing of wild ways, no one can graph the movements of the searun cutthroat with absolute authority. It remains a mystery fish, here today and gone tomorrow—if not sooner.

That mercurial quality is part of the magic that set its hooks in me on the day I glimpsed my first cutthroat. I was a small boy then. We—which is to say my mother, father, sister Shirley and I—were rolling west by Canadian Pacific railway train on yet another of the gypsyings that mark a small-church minister's existence. The train ground its way over a bridge. On the far side, waiting for the train to pass, stood a boy in overalls. In one hand he held an alder pole, in the other a string of gleaming fish threaded on a greenwood crotch. As our car passed, the boy held up his catch and gave us a gap-toothed grin. That flash, that revelation of bright bold-speckled trout, remained vivid in memory.

These, then, were the fish that invaded our river on that evening of watery sunlight after a three-day August rain. The

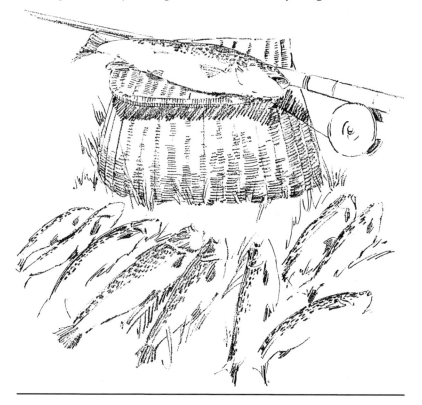

water, though it still ran brown, was rapidly clearing. Anchored knee deep with the swollen current shoving hard against my legs, I cast again, and on the instant my fly was assaulted.

Besides being unsophisticated, those cutties were charged with all the dash and ginger that a saltwater sojourn imparts. They struck hard and fought like crazy, often throwing themselves clear of the water in straight-up leaps that rattled their gill plates.

We caught trout until our arms were tired. Conservation in those days was less than a whisper on the wind. Bag limits were generous. Even so, this wholesale slaughter of worthy fish palled on us. We began releasing our trout.

When my father had fed his last worm to the ravening horde, he continued to hook trout on the bare spinner. I left the last of my flies in the jaw of a great bruiser that smashed at it in four inches of water. Weary, for once satiated, we turned back to camp. If not the best day's fishing my father and I ever shared, that was most certainly the wildest.

At the little forestry park we found that another car, a boxy tan Essex, had pulled in. A lean man with a clipped mustache and a woman in khaki breeches were setting up an umbrella tent grander far than our frayed, patched and once-white wall tent. Two small girls watched from their perch on a park table. An older girl was laying out tent pegs from a bag. Her brown legs were bare; she wore a tan skirt and a white blouse. Her curly hair was either light brown or dark gold, I couldn't be sure which. She gave me an impersonal glance, then bent her head to her job.

I had become aware of girls in this last year or two, but I was shy with them. I wasn't too sure that I liked sharing our campground, which we had come to consider our private preserve, with one of the species. It never occurred to me as I trudged past with flyrod in hand that fate had brushed me with a wingtip.

9.
Year of the Girl

ARMY LIFE, FOLLOWED BY HIS YEARS as minister to small starveling churches, had turned my father into a make-do artist and a peerless scrounger. These gifts were never more apparent than when we were setting up our camp. Our eight-by-ten wall tent of untreated canvas was the nucleus of our caravanserai. As a first step, we would ransack the cross-river woods for saplings to give us ridgepole and twin A-frames, one for each end. But the wall tent was only a beginning.

Next Dad would cast about for ways by which he could improve the quality of an outdoor existence. On this particular year—the year of the girl—he backed blarney with a gift of trout to persuade a highways crew to provide our camp with a kitchen. This was a roofed but open-sided shelter from the other end of the campground. The cheerful highways men uprooted its corner posts and shifted it roof and all to be reinstalled facing into our tent mouth.

From this point Dad took over. Nosing about in the wreckage of an abandoned shack across the highway, he came on a rusted sheet-metal stove of the sort favoured by foresters and sheep-herders. We slung it on a pole, padded our shoulders with our rolled jackets, and marched the stove across to our new kitchen. There Dad established it in a log crib filled with sand fetched up toilsomely from the river bucket by bucket. He then lit a fire in the firebox, and while the stove was heating, gave it a rubdown with bacon grease, a refinement that improved its appearance no end.

We improvised cupboards and shelves from canned milk boxes, also scavenged, which we spiked to the corner posts. As a final touch we gave our kitchen more substance by lashing our tarp to make walls for two sides. That night, with our stove cherry red and ourselves perched on firewood rounds in front of it, we enjoyed a degree of comfort not experienced before.

One evening a few days later, just after the stately Essex had brought us our new neighbours, I left Dad to plan a means of piping water from the ravine spring into our kitchen. Curious to learn whether those invading searuns had ventured farther into fresh water, I set out with rod in hand. A couple of hundred yards below the highway bridge, a tangle of freshet-piled logs had jammed in an elbow of the stream. One result of this partial blockage was an interesting pool that gave us the occasional fish.

I took up station in the entrance riffle, and was drifting a fly down to the deeper water when a flicker of movement on the logjam caught my eye. The curly-haired girl in the tan skirt and white blouse was perched on a sun-dried log.

I gave her a grudging flip of my hand. She offered a perfunctory wave in return, then centred her attention on the book in her lap.

A book? A girl who read for pleasure? This was something new under the sun. I was a voracious reader myself, devouring everything from comics to my father's sober-sided and church-oriented *Homiletic Review.* Curiosity battled with shyness and won out. I waded the riffle and edged along the log toward the girl.

"What are you reading?" I asked her.

"*Black Bartlemy's Treasure,*" she said, not looking up.

"Jeffery Farnol," I said. "I read it, too. It's a good one."

She looked up at me then, eyebrows arched in surprise. A boy who read, and was willing to admit it, was a rare bird.

We fell to talking, first about books we'd read, then about ourselves. Her name was Winifred. She was thirteen years old, a mere child compared to my sixteen years. But we met as equals, and neither then nor later did we indulge in the boy-girl charade of "putting on an act." This was a voyage of discovery. We talked while the light deepened, then strolled back along the riverbank trail to camp. At first sight, I had thought her plain. But she wasn't, I realized now. Win was pretty, with her high forehead and grey eyes and gentle mouth.

We were still talking when we sat by the campfire her people had lit. They were amused. So was my father, who joined us in the circle of firelight. They were no more aware than we that a strong alchemy was at work.

I turned in that night in a muddle of mixed emotions. I had found not merely a girl but a friend such as I'd never had before. Someone I could talk to and confide in. The discovery was earth-shaking.

For the rest of Win's stay, we were inseparable. She went fishing with me. We swam in a bridge pool with gravel bottom and limestone ledges showing clear in the late-summer low that had shrunk my river. We picked sweet little wild blackberries in the burn, with Win's two small sisters tagging along.

On the last evening before Win left, we perched on the downstream logjam in silence intruded upon only by the muted river song. For the first time in three weeks, we were not talking.

Finally I asked. "Will you come back next year?"

"I don't know," Win said. "I hope so."

Next morning, glumly, I watched the Essex recede down the highway.

My father got his strayed fishing partner back. We wound up our stay and returned to Vancouver for another humdrum year.

Next August, and the one after that, Win and I picked up our friendship as if we'd never been parted. But a shadow hung over the third year of our shared holidays. We knew it would be our last. I would have to find work next summer to finance my first university year. Win, a better student than I ever was, would be through high school and also looking for a job.

We had not met or tried to meet in the city. Here by the river we could enjoy an uncomplicated friendship as equals. In Vancouver all was different. I lived in the tough and shabby East End. Win's home was on a good street in smart Kerrisdale. Her people were well fixed. Mine struggled along on a bare-bones salary that never at any time in my father's years as a minister exceeded a hundred and fifty dollars a month. In Win's far different world there were other boys: smart dressers, sophisticates, some with cars, all sure of themselves and their futures. The odds, I convinced myself, were too heavy against me.

On our last evening we went for a walk along one of the old logging grades. Shadows were lengthening. Below us, across an alder-grown flat, the river trailed its silver ribbon through the dusk. Win turned into my arms and I kissed her. That kiss, our first, was both hello and goodbye. It was three mortal years before we met again.

By that time I was in my junior year at the University of British Columbia. The Depression had the land in its iron grip, but I'd been lucky; from April into September of each year, I worked in an upcoast logging camp. It was a good, tough, physical life and it kept me where I preferred to be, which was outdoors. I had done my determined best to put Win out of my mind. She was not for me.

One day at the heel of a wet and dreary coast winter, I looked up from the loading platform of a downtown tramline as a streetcar pulled in. Through the window above me, I saw a fair remembered face. My heart lurched. It was Win. My instant impression was that she looked worried and sad. Then the car moved on, and I was left to realize that nothing had changed, nothing had been forgotten. I hadn't succeeded in putting Win out of my mind.

I wrote her a letter. No answer came. Then one evening, when I'd given up hope of hearing from her, she phoned. She'd been away visiting with friends. And, yes, if I still wanted to, we could meet—maybe go for a walk in Stanley Park.

The weeks that followed were strange ones. We tried to pick up our uncomplicated friendship, but too much had changed for that. We were older. Win's father, a civil engineer, had been laid off, and the family had fallen on hard times. Also, as I learned with a stab of jealousy, there was another boy in the picture, one with marriage on his mind.

April came, and with it my summons from the Loggers' Agency. My job was waiting. I was to pick up my papers and board the Union Steamships coaster *Chelohsin* that midnight. There was time for only the briefest farewells. Win and I parted with nothing settled and not even a hint that we would see each other again. I wrote from the outpost shack where I was stationed on fire patrol and got a constrained and discouragingly formal answer. Then, while the weeks dragged past, no answer to my further letters.

Each mail day after work, I would hike the twelve miles to the logging camp in hopes of a reply, to tramp back through the dark empty-handed. This until one day in early September when I put in at the camp commissary to find that a letter had come for me. It was in Win's handwriting. I shoved it in my hip pocket, not daring to open it for fear of what it might tell me.

Finally, halfway to my shack at the end of the railway steel, I halted on a siding where a string of skeleton cars had been spotted to wait until a locomotive could position them alongside a log-loading brow. I climbed onto one of the cars, settled myself on one of the bunks, and fished the crumpled letter from my pocket. It would be bad news. It would inform me that she intended to marry the other fellow.

Alone in brilliant moonlight, steeled for the worst, I opened her letter. The word was not what I feared. She had been thinking of me, hoping I would soon come home. When I did, would I like to call around at her house?

A dragging week later, I toted packsack and suitcase on to the little *Chelohsin*, southbound for town. The ship was crammed with loggers bound down to Vancouver for a blowout. I won a box of chocolates on a ship lottery, and yearned to keep it as a gift for Win. But the loggers' code as it touched on such matters was inflexible. What you won, you shared. So I watched my chocolates disappear, and instead bought Win a little carved totem pole on a silver chain.

I called at her home the next night, burned almost black by the logging country sun and awkward in the first town clothes worn since spring. We went for a walk. I gave Win the totem, which she slipped around her neck. In the course of our walk we came to an understanding, to use a quaint old term, and we have never looked back since.

I did not return to university that fall, nor did I accept the junior management job the logging company had offered me at Franklin River. Instead I followed my bent and pestered the Vancouver *Daily Province* into giving me a berth as a space writer paid by the column inch for his gleanings. A few months later, the management realized that I was racking up considerably more on space than a junior reporter's meagre salary, and offered me a staff job at five dollars a week less than I'd been making.

During that time I met one of our greatest writers and a splendid fisherman. In an outdoor column for the *Province,* I asked a question — I think it had to do with the use of the dry fly for searun cutthroat — and I got a scholarly and obviously knowledgeable answer from someone who signed his name Roderick Haig-Brown and gave his address as Campbell River. We kept in touch by letter although we never met.

Then one rainy day about two years after that first letter, a youngish man in a stained old trench coat came into the *Province* newsroom with a parcel under his arm and inquired his way to my desk. He opened his parcel, and in it were the two original volumes of his first major work, *The Western Angler.* He explained quite apologetically that he couldn't give me the books, that they were in short supply, but that he thought that I would appreciate reading them, and possibly I could write a review of them. I jumped at the chance. I reviewed them for the Province, and I suppose that deepened a friendship already started.

It was a curious sort of friendship. We'd meet only rarely. When we did we'd get along very well indeed. Strangely, though we were both keen fly fishermen, we never got the opportunity to fish together. Time and circumstance, I suppose; it just never worked out that way.

He was a man who did things with grace, a quiet man who tended to seek the shade. He was a natural woodsman, perhaps partly because of his boyhood training in England; he was brought up in the shooting and fishing tradition as the son of country gentry. As a fisherman he had few equals. He approached fishing both as a scientist and as an artist; he made a deep study of it. He originated a number of different flies, notably some salmon fry imitations that are very appealing to searun cutthroat trout. He went a long way toward pioneering fly fishing for winter steelhead with a fly. Previous to Haig-Brown's time it was generally believed that winter steelhead could not be caught on a fly, but he demonstrated that they could be. He treated them like the Atlantic salmon of the English waters that he grew up on.

Secure now with a salaried job at the *Province,* and at least marginally solvent, I did two things I'd wanted to do. I bought my girl an engagement ring, and since it would be as well for our future if she learned to fish, I emptied my bank account to set her up with a beautiful little Hardy Triumph flyrod complete with reel and line, leaders and flies.

"He had the ring box in one hand," Win remembers, "and the flyrod in the other. I took it as an ultimatum."

Win accepted both ring and rod. The ring is still on her finger, and the Hardy Triumph, in spite of a long, arduous and honourable career, is still as straight as when she first uncased its gleaming sections.

10.

Cutthroat Heaven

Big JIM TAYLOR WAS A HAUNTED MAN. One of a band of
heroes who had fought the terrible Merville fire of 1922, he
could never free his mind of what he had seen and experienced.

One apple-green dusk, sitting with my father and me on the
verandah of Fishermen's Lodge which he ran, Jim told how he
and another firefighter had been trapped between walls of flame.
They had sheltered in a pool of Black Creek. As the fire closed
in, Jim's companion went mad. He rushed out into the hotspot.
Jim, only his face above surface, watched him flare like a torch
before he collapsed, a blackened horror, into the fire. The fire
vaulted the creek and marched on. Jim crept out of his hole,
parboiled but alive, with memories to bear that he would gladly
have buried.

Now, hunched over his knees on the verandah step with the
Oyster River murmuring at his back, he gazed into the darkening
north.

"There's one hell of a big one coming," he predicted. "It'll
be even bigger than the Merville."

Jim was no false prophet. The 1938 Sayward Fire, when it
boiled out of logging country to the northwest and charged
down-island with a hot summer wind to hurry it along, proved
to be the biggest woods fire that our British Columbia coast has
ever suffered. At its peak it was ten miles wide and forty long. It

destroyed millions of dollars worth of felled and standing timber and logging gear. Four towns — Campbell River, Courtenay, Cumberland and Bevan — were threatened. No wild creature lived to stir in the desert left by its passing. Even my river, which stood in its way but failed to check its advance, suffered most cruelly.

As a junior reporter for the Vancouver *Daily Province* I was assigned to help a senior man, the great Torchy Anderson, to cover the monstrous blaze. This was an experience in itself. Once I found myself away out on what was more a fire trail than a road, with my poor little car bogged down and the fire moving briskly through the slash toward me. Luckily, a crew of firefighters came staggering out of the woods, all smoke-blackened. They simply picked up my car and turned it around end for end. We got out of there together with the firefighters clinging to every conceivable part of the car.

Torchy was a splendid reporter, and I feel still that he was the best newspaper man that British Columbia ever produced. He was a legend in his own time. At the time he was the star reporter for the Vancouver *Daily Province,* and it was my great good fortune to be teamed up with him as his junior.

Torchy was a big burly man, broad and heavy and tall. He could wear his hats with an indescribable air. No other reporter managed to get quite the curve into the brim of a snap-brim hat that Torchy did. He was violently freckled. He had a rather pugnacious way with him, although he could be very gentle, very diplomatic too. He was completely fearless, and especially when he was on a story he'd bore right in and damn the torpedoes. His name came from his short-fused temper. He would not stand for much nonsense before blowing his top. When he was angry — which wasn't often — the results were quite spectacular. His voice would climb to a high squeal. When you heard that high squeal it was just as well to take cover.

I was deeply fond of Torchy. He was more than my mentor.

He was my friend and my fishing partner. We fished many times together. One of my fondest memories is seeing a blizzard of snow close in on Torchy one March day on the Harrison River. It masked him completely from sight, and then the blizzard whirled away, and there was Torchy still laying out a long line and a light fly.

In the course of covering the Sayward Fire, I put in at my father's camp in the forestry park. He had a tale to tell.

"When the fire got so close I could see the flames," he told me over dinner, "I decided I'd better clear out. So I bundled up my camp cot and went down to the river mouth. It was black as the inside of a cow except for the glare in the sky upstream. Anyway, I set up my cot on the beach and went to sleep."

Dad dished out second helpings of his specialty corned beef hash. "Well," he went on, "sometime in the night I woke feeling cold underneath. I put a hand over the side of the cot and felt water. Turned out I'd rigged my cot on the tideflats in the dark, and the tide had come in."

When the fire was over, I took my vacation. I pointed myself like a homing dove for the river, and arrived to be met by my father. His face was doleful.

"Look at the river," he bade me.

I did, and it was running red with soil washed down from the great scar the fire had left in its wake.

"It's been like that for a week," Dad said.

A white oval showed in the red. It was a trout, a big one, floating belly-up in the silt-laden current.

"The river's taken a beating," Dad said gloomily. "I just hope it'll come back."

Come back it did, though not that year. Our favourite pools and runs remained barren. The only area where we could pick up the occasional trout was in the estuary where salt water mingled with fresh, and even there, the fishing remained poor.

One blue and gold morning, Dad and I fished our way

down to the estuary without so much as a touch. Beyond its flanking bars, the melding of the river with the saltchuck was marked by a pinkish stain. We cinched up our waders and worked our way out past the tip of the south bar. The shallows ran a long way into the Strait of Georgia. By the time I halted, cold water was trickling in at the top of my boots. We were committed to the sea, surrounded by it, with the shore distant behind us.

Dad in his chest waders was still farther out, exploring the last of the river current with looping casts of his worm and spinner. I worked out line myself and laid a slim-tied Peter Ross, a bright confection of barred teal wing and silver and red body, slantwise across the gentle flow.

Absorbed in fishing the fly, I paid no attention to Dad until his actions became so untoward as to compel notice. Rod held high, gaze riveted on the water, he was backing up one slow step after another.

"Hey," I called to him across the water-gap. "What's up?"

In a taut voice he answered my hail. "I've got company."

At that point, a large, dark and infinitely sinister shadow lazed through the water until it was only a foot or so from my boots. Now I knew what my father meant.

"Shark?" I called.

"Big one," he answered. "There's more around." He eased another step closer to the hopelessly distant-seeming bar, and offered hoarse-voiced advice. "Keep moving—slow—"

Our shoreward passage seemed to take forever. And with each cautious backward shuffle, our grim escort kept pace with us.

We were used to the sharks' little cousins, the three-foot dogfish with their emerald eyes and underslung jaws. These, emphatically, were not dogfish. Torpedo-shaped, sleek and streamlined, the brute all but nosing my leg looked to be at least eight feet long. Dad's course and mine converged until we were moving side by side. So were our attendants, following us faithfully as paired shadows.

We made it to knee depth. We took another step backward, and twin monstrous swirls boiled in front of us. The two sharks, having tagged us in until they all but grounded, had turned seaward away from us.

In a cold sweat, I splashed out to the welcome safety of the bar. I'd been scared silly. Dad held out his hands: they were trembling.

"What kind were they?" I asked in a voice that emerged as a croak.

"I don't know," Dad said. He gave his shoulders a shake. "I don't want to know."

Perhaps they belonged to an inshore breed called salmon sharks. We never saw their kind again, but never again did I feel entirely comfortable while deep-wading in the estuary.

For Dad, the sharks put a stopper to a day which was not one of our best. He trudged back up the river toward camp. I lingered, squatting on the bar with flyrod leaned against a knee. It was a fine rod, my Kohinor, but I could take no pleasure from it today.

I was worried about Dad. It had not been the best of years for him. Early on, a flareup of one of his old war wounds had put him in Shaughnessy Military Hospital. No sooner was he discharged than he learned that his salary—meagre enough, Lord knows—had been cut to meet the Depression's harsh necessities.

Then one evening, as he walked home alone through Hastings Park from a pastoral call, a man stepped out of pavement-bordering brush and poked a handgun into his ribs. Dad's reaction was instant and automatic. He half turned, shoved the gun arm violently aside, and with fist cocked, stepped inside the thug's guard.

A terrified squeak checked his hand. "Mister Mayse—I'm sorry—I didn't know it was you!"

Dad recognized the voice and pop-eyed face as belonging to a young man of his congregation. He reached out and took the gun—which proved to be a cap pistol—from a shaking hand.

"Howard," he said sternly, "I'm ashamed of you. This won't do."

The boy was another victim of the Depression. Unable to find work, the harebrained loon had decided to go on the pad. But his luck was out, or perhaps in, for my father was his first prospect. Dad took him sobbing home and turned him over to his people. Like fools they spread the story around, and the inevitable pastor-hating faction pounced on it. Justice must be served. Why hadn't my father done his duty and turned the miscreant over to the police? And so on.

Meanwhile deeper trouble developed. A new church was in process of building, the funds provided largely by the Board of Home Missions. As the work proceeded, my father became aware that all was not as it should be. The brick pile meant for the chimney kept diminishing. Lumber stacks shrank. One night, in the shadows of the unfinished vestry, my father kept watch for the thieves.

In the early hours, a truck turned into the side street. The driver doused his lights and pussyfooted his vehicle down to the new church site. There he hopped out, unloaded a wheelbarrow, and began to transfer bricks from pile to truck. Dad, moving softly, eased out with the intention of confronting the thief. But he caught his toe on a loose two-by-four, which clattered across the floor.

Alerted, the fellow bolted for his truck, but not before Dad glimpsed and recognized the rat face of a congregation member. Red-hot mad, Dad called a meeting of church officers, before whom the thief was summoned. He denied all, and since there was no evidence to go on except my father's unsupported word, the charge was not pressed. More bad blood. More factionalism, not helped by my father's inability to play the diplomat. He was a blunt man who favoured plain speaking; he trod on toes and offended sensibilities, and those whose toes he trampled whetted their knives for him. It was obvious that Dad's days as shepherd of the cross-grained flock were numbered.

Brooding over all this, worried and restless, I was in no mood to return to camp. Instead, I forded the river at the first upstream riffle and plodded north along the sea beach. With the estuary out of sight behind a timbered point, I found a little bay with gently curving shoreline. It was a wild and blessedly lonely reach, its shore littered with bleached drift and dominated by silver-grey snags and stumps that had journeyed down the river on the last freshet. Across the Strait of Georgia, the fantastic jumble of mainland mountains lifted powder-blue in the after-noon haze.

I lowered myself to the sunwarmed shingle, set my back against a drift log, and was settling in for a little shut-eye when an abrupt splash impinged on my ears. I sat up and looked out to the bay. An inshore kelp bed poked its shiny brown bulbs through the surface a matter of a hundred feet from the beach. In the lee of the kelp, I saw a circle of spreading rings.

Salmon, I decided. A coho chasing minnows. But I got up, reached my rod from where it leaned against a stump, and strolled over shingle and wave-smoothed stones to the water's edge. Before my boots were in the water, a swirl humped the glassy surface between kelp and shore, and another set of rings began to spread.

Heart thumping, I waded in, pulled line off my reel and laid out a cast with my Kohinor, which made nothing of a sixty-foot throw. The leader uncurled, the fly—that same Peter Ross— ducked beneath the surface. I began to recover line in a series of easy pulls.

A travelling bulge showed astern of my fly. It followed— followed—followed—then expanded into a swirl. On the in-stant, I felt a rude snatch at my fly. For a moment, from the way the fish ripped line off my screeching reel, I thought I was into a coho. But the run stopped short of the coho's two-hundred-foot dash, and the broad side that flashed yellow through clear water did not belong to any salmon.

Cutthroat! I was tethered to the biggest searun I'd ever hooked in my life.

Why draw out tragedy? After a quarter hour of give and take, the lunges became less powerful, each run shorter than the last. Then, without warning, the great cutty charged straight at my feet. Desperately, I strove to recover the loose line. But a loop flipped around a button of my fishing vest, and on that instant, the fish took off on another run. It was a weak and weary effort, but it sufficed. The loop tightened. The leader snapped. The searun cutthroat of a lifetime swam free.

I hooked and landed two more

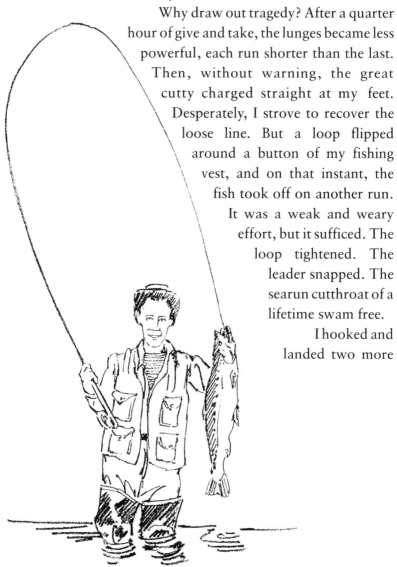

trout, good ones, but they couldn't compensate for the one that got away. Even so, and in spite of my disappointment, I realized that I had stumbled on what every searun cutthroat aficionado hopes to find: a beach removed from fresh water where searuns congregate, lured by good feeding, for most months of the year.

I told my father about the discovery, and backed my story with a brace of handsome cutties. Dad brightened considerably. When I took him there on next morning's low tide and he caught his first searun in a week of trying, he became once more his old self.

"This place deserves a name, Bill," he said. "Why don't we call it Cutthroat Heaven?"

We did, and the name remains.

11.

The Silent Partners

A MAN IN WILD COUNTRY can convince himself that he is utterly alone, and so he may be in terms of human company. But there are other presences, other eyes watching. Masters of this planet we may be, but we share it with an infinite variety of creatures.

A fisherman, and particularly a stream fisherman for trout, is more likely than most to encounter these other inhabitants. He bends, he blurs, he belongs to the scene. His colours are rarely obtrusive. His movements almost always are unhurried, and he stands motionless for considerable spaces except for the to-and-fro of his casting arm.

Take my father, for instance, on a day when we had followed our river several miles upstream from the highway bridge. He was working his way down a long, gently flowing glide, dropping his worm-and-spinner into the alder-shaded pockets that searun cutthroat favour on their upriver pilgrimages. Always a deep wader, he was out almost to the top of his boots when of a sudden he began to conduct himself in a most curious and alarming manner. He staggered. He lunged forward with wildly waving rod. Then he wallowed toward the bar at as close to a run as a man in chest waders can manage through water. Arrived, he slipped down his wader suspenders, meanwhile shuffling his feet in an erratic little dance. With the waders bagging around his knees, he cast himself down on the shingle.

"Help me off with them," he ordered. "Hurry!"

I grabbed his boot-feet and hauled. The waders peeled off. Out of them crawled a large, annoyed garter snake, which promptly glided into the shelter of a tag alder stand. Our conjecture: the snake, wounded by hawk or raven, had either been dropped into the river or had taken to it for refuge. It had been sidewinding its way down with the current when it fetched up against Dad's waders. It had slithered into their shelter — after all, there was only an inch or two of freeboard remaining — and when it realized its mistake, had set up a frantic squirming.

We have no venomous snakes on Vancouver Island, and are also free of the short-fused and unpredictable grizzly bear. Our two large predators, the black bear and the cougar, powerful beasts well equipped for mayhem, molest humans so rarely that an attack makes front page news. The cougar or mountain lion, however, is of a divided nature. He is constitutionally wary of man and his works. At the same time, the insatiable curiosity which he shares with his cousin the house cat can prod him into recklessness, or following a foot traveller alone on a night trail.

Seasoned bushwhackers don't take much stock in cougars, though they'll go out of their way to avoid a meeting

with a black bear. The consensus is that only a brash young cat or an arthritic oldster with worn-down teeth would ever present a threat to a human. Even then, the object of attack was far more likely to be a small child than a grownup. One old woods-rat added a proviso. If you're travelling a cougar country trail in early morning dusk or evening twilight, don't sit or lie down to rest. Ease your packboard against stump or tree if you must, but stay on your feet. Erect, you retain your human identity, and are not to be trifled with lightly.

Cougar depredations seem to go in waves. Things are quiet for a few years. Then there seems to be a cougar behind every bush; a child or two is attacked, dogs are vacuumed up, cats disappear, and people are frightened. The cougar population multiplies, and man's inroads have drastically reduced the black-tail deer population. Hungry large meat-eating animals, deprived of their natural food, go hunting for something to eat. This brings them down to the edges of settlements, sometimes right into settlements.

Strange though it may seem, the chances of seeing a cougar are considerably better today than they were back when the big cats had a price on their heads. Today, few hunters court the brutally hard foot-slogging through the wet snow of the winter boondocks that treeing a cougar entails. In earlier years, bounty hunters systematically wiped out every cougar and kit they could lay their sights on. Famed predator control officer Cecil "Cougar" Smith, acting under government orders, singlehan-dedly reduced the Upper Island population by well over nine hundred cougar. As a matter of fact, our present house at Stories Beach was earlier bought by Cougar Smith with bounty dollars.

My sole attempt to claim a forty-dollar cougar bounty—a sum about equal to my take-home pay for the month—ended in humiliation. Near the logging camp where I worked was a lake, and down to this lake on an occasional spring evening strolled a large cougar, probably a female. Her route was along a windfall fir that spanned a belt of skunk cabbage marsh to slope into the water.

The cougar in those years was considered vermin rather than a game animal protected by closed seasons and regulations. I borrowed a rifle and a few cartridges from a chokerman friend. The piece was a ponderous old Steyr military arm, a nine-millimetre if I remember correctly, which had been reduced to carbine length by the crude expedient of sawing a hunk off its barrel. The noses of the steel jackets on the thumb-sized cartridges had been filed through in a cross-shaped pattern so the lead would mushroom on impact.

That evening, early, I stationed myself on a windfall trunk of my own that bridged the black mud of the swamp, across a narrow inlet from the cougar's catwalk. Crouched there with rifle ready, I waited. Evening deepened into dusk. Another quarter-hour and visibility would be too poor to get in a shot. Still no cougar. Maybe I'd picked the wrong night.

Then, like magic, there was the cougar. She paced daintily down the log. Where the lake water lapped it, she glanced around, casing the layout no doubt, then lowered her head and began to drink. Balanced on my tree trunk, elbows on knees, I lined up on what should have been an easy shot. I eased back on the trigger . . . and all hell broke loose. Off the trunk I tumbled, propelled by a kick from the Steyr that would have done justice to a mule, to land on my back among the skunk cabbages. There I floundered with ears still ringing, until I could collect my wits and exhume myself and the villainous old fusil from the mud bath.

Where the slug went, I have no idea. But the cougar had pulled her vanishing act. After all, what cat in its right mind would linger for an encore of such a performance? My verdict, delivered to myself while laboriously getting the mud off and out of the borrowed rifle: Serves you damned well right!

Cougar Smith in those days was on assignment from the fish and game department to reduce the cougar population of northern Vancouver Island. Then he was called a bonus hunter in the employ of the government; today he would be called a predator control officer.

One of the jokes about Cougar Smith was that he led his dogs to the cougars, rather than the reverse, because his dogs were worthless. In fact he had some very good dogs, but they were the wildest mix of breeds. In the front bedroom of our house, the house he bought with his bounty money, we have a picture of him with a couple of his dogs. One looks to be an English sheepdog with hair all over its eyes, and the other is a nondescript mutt of some kind.

Cougar Smith was a terrific woodsman, but he had some peculiarities. Since he hated to be caught in the woods after dark, he would make fantastic journeys through the roughest kind of country to get home for the night. The evening I met him, that's precisely what he was doing. I was up covering the single unemployed camps of the Thirties, and I was on my way back from the Elk Falls camp with the forestry man who was my guide. We came on a truck beside the road with its lights off. We pulled in to see if someone was in trouble, as was the neighbourly custom in those years, and here was Cougar Smith catching a little doze in the cab. My forestry friend introduced me, and we had a pleasant chat. He was a courteous, quiet-spoken man. He showed us his bag of two large cougar tossed into the back of the truck before we went our way.

Dad and I were followed several times by cougars. A minor rustle in the brush parallel to the trail—the glimmer of one gooseberry-green eye—these were the signs of a watcher in the woods. Once in snow time on a steelhead fishing jaunt we backtracked our footsteps to find them overlaid for a quarter-mile or so with cougar imprints.

Again, Win and I once found cougar tracks on a sand patch no more than twelve feet from our camp on the riverbank. The story was plain. One set of prints was large, the other small: a mother and her this-year's kit had passed that way in the night. Next night we waited up, swathed in our sleeping bags, hoping to catch a moonlight glimpse of the pair. But our observation post was comfortable and the night mild. We fell asleep, not to wake until full morning. Fresh tracks showed in the sand. Not only had mama and youngling passed this way again; they had obviously paused to give us a thorough looking-over.

The black bear, which enjoys the reputation of being a harmless, roly-poly woods clown, will most times take off in high gear at the approach of a man. But not always, and this makes him a creature best avoided. Not that avoidance is always possible, as Win and I found out while strolling the Island Highway just north of Oyster River bridge.

We had been to a farm for eggs. Our way back to camp led past a densely wooded tract. As we passed, Win said, "I saw something black in there." Knowing I was deathly afraid of cattle, she decided to have a little fun with me. "It looked to me like a big black bull."

At this point, Mister Big-and-Black charged out of the woods. He was hitting on all cylinders, his hind feet overlapping his front paws at every stride. Our bag of brown country eggs landed on the blacktop with a melancholy *plop*. A black bear — the largest black bear these startled eyes have ever looked on — bolted across the highway so close to us that he all but knocked Win off her feet. Across the highway, a cutbank offered an approach to the logging burn. We stood there absolutely petrified, too amazed to be frightened. It was a truly monstrous black bear. The bear, a six-hundred-pounder at the very least, hurled himself at the cutbank with a great scrabbling of hind paws. The unstable gravel slid, and the bear with it, to tumble head over heels at its foot. He picked himself up, made a second more successful attempt, and vanished into the burn. We were left, shaken, to salvage what we could of our eggs.

The bear, we gathered later, was a notorious sheep-stealer. Gorged with mutton after a raid on Walter Woodhus's flock, it had been lurking in the roadside timber, getting up its nerve for the traverse of the highway. Once launched, it was blind to anything between it and its goal.

Time passed. The raids on Walter's sheep continued. Traps, poison and stakeouts with a buckshot-charged shotgun failed to halt Bruin's depredations. Then one murky autumn night, Walter burst into the Fishermen's Lodge beer parlour which was the social centre for this outlying community.

Walter was in a state. "Boys," he announced in a hoarse and quaking voice, "I just hit a man with my truck. Couldn't see him proper — he was wearing a long fur coat. He's laying out there in the brush."

The patrons boiled out of the beer parlour to investigate. What they discovered by the uncertain glimmer of a flashlight was not a man in a long fur coat but a very large dead-as-a-doornail black bear. Significantly, Walter's woollies suffered no further attacks.

Domestic animals gone half wild, such as the cattle that Oyster River farmers allowed to range freely upriver, also presented a hazard. One bull known as Two-Ton Tony was legendary for his ferocious attacks on unwary hunters and fishermen.

One day upriver, pleased with good fishing, we were making the long trek down to camp. We had just emerged from the cool green depths of an alder swamp to the open burn when a monstrous apparition loomed before us among the stumps. It was black as sin and big as a mountain, and a glance under its belly revealed it to be an indubitable bull.

Still as a statue carved from ebony, it glowered at us.

Dad's voice sounded quietly from beside me. "Ease over to those stumps," he ordered. "Drop everything and climb one."

The bull, as if to lend emphasis to his words, pawed with one massive hoof. Red logging country soil puffed into the air.

I sidled toward a tall stump, blessing the earlier loggers for their wastefulness in felling their trees well above the swell of the butt. Out of the corner of my eye, I could see my father slipping his creel strap and leaning his rod against another stump.

In complete and deathly silence, the bull lowered its head and charged. I went up my stump like a monkey, fear propelling me. The springboard notches axed into the stump by the fallers offered footholds. Perched atop my refuge, I saw Dad swing himself safely aboard his stump top. Below, the bull regarded us with an evil eye. Then, to show what it would do to us if we came down, it horned my stump so that the rotten surface duff crumbled away.

"Don't worry," Dad called to me. "We're safe." He scowled down at the broad back and wicked horns. "What I'd give to have my shotgun!" he growled.

"You think this is Two-Ton Tony?" I asked, trying to keep the quaver out of my voice.

Two-Ton Tony had rousted any number of fishermen and

bird hunters. His hide was stuck full of bird shot as a ham with cloves, and the mere sight of a man touched off his hair-trigger temper.

"Not this runt," Dad called back. "Two-Ton Tony's twice as big."

Hours passed. The heat became sweltering, a fact that I noted to my father.

"Just be glad it's not raining," he told me grimly.

The sun was westering when salvation, in the shape of a little band of wild cows, drifted toward us among the stumps. They grazed their way past. The bull, torn in two directions, made his choice. He gave us one more look — I noticed incongruously that he had straw-coloured eyelashes — then his eagerness for female company overcame his desire to horn and trample the bejudas out of us. He traipsed off after the cows. We gave him a quarter-hour to remove himself from our vicinity, then descended stiffly from our stumps, collected rods and creel, and with frequent and fearful glances over our shoulders, headed for camp.

Years later I got the final word on Two-Ton Tony's lurid story from a Courtenay man. A couple of autumns after our run-in with the lesser bull, Two-Ton Tony surprised a grouse hunter who had paused in the shadow of a stump to dress his birds.

The hunter squirrelled his way to safety, escaping Two-Ton Tony's horns by a hair. From his life-saving stump, he then watched the monster stomp his cherished shotgun, an English Purdy no less, into shattered wood and twisted metal.

But this time the bully had picked the wrong victim. The hunter, a militiaman, returned to Courtenay with a yearning for vengeance in his heart. He rounded up several militia chums. Next Sunday, armed with Sten guns and plenty of ammo, they invaded the burn. They found Two-Ton Tony — or more likely he found them — and squirted the old devil full of lead. On the theory that he was too tough even for hamburger, they left his carcass to the ravens.

Wild dogs could also be terrifying. When I worked on a logging camp fire patrol, a blacksmith at one of the beach camps left his two Great Danes behind to fend for themselves when the camp closed. It was a heartless act. The big dogs did as animals left to their own devices must, and turned wild, foraging for deer. They haunted the area that I and my partner Paddy Gorman patrolled, and they made our job really dangerous. Several times they jumped us, and we lived in terror of them. Once they kept me up on a cold-deck pile of logs for most of an afternoon before they got tired of waiting for me to come down and wandered off.

We were patrolling a remote valley in the claim where the trees had been taken down but not yet yarded out on the railway. This was the valley the dogs haunted. One evening when we were sitting on the back steps of our bunkhouse, a railway car that had been run to the end of the railway spur, we could hear the dogs giving tongue away off in the distance. We realized they were running a deer down a draw that came out and crossed the spur a little more than two hundred yards from our bunkhouse. Just on the off chance I went and got my rifle. It was a Winchester 1894 carbine, a nice little gun, but with an effective range of only roughly a hundred and fifty yards. I got sitting on the back step with my elbows on my knees and the rifle cocked, a very comfortable position, and waited.

The dogs' voices came closer and closer, and finally a fine buck burst out of the slash where the draw tapered down to the railway track. It had been run hard and it was staggering. It kept on going across the railway tracks and presently, as we expected, one of the dogs burst into view. I led the dog just as though I was shooting at a flying duck, and touched off, and he went cartwheeling end over end. I'd made a fluke shot. The other dog showed itself, then vanished. We went out to investigate the dead dog with the rifle ready. It was a fearsome beast, a wild animal, no longer a tame dog. Its mate must have left that part of the country, because we never saw it again. I don't boast about this, because nobody likes to admit to killing a dog.

Once in a while, comedy does brighten nature's prevailingly sombre scene. Walter Woodhus was a fine generous man, one of the typical old-timers as I've been lucky enough to know them. He was also an inspired tale-spinner, and one of his favourite haunts was the Oyster River beer parlour. One night there we got talking about the salmon runs, and someone bewailed the fact that the runs were considerably diminished. Walter joined in the mourning. He was silent for a thoughtful moment, then said, "You know, I remember once the salmon in that river almost killed me." Then he was quiet, and applied himself to his beer.

Finally somebody asked how this had happened. Walter said that once a couple of federal fisheries men wanted to make a salmon count. They chose a long open river reach with a top riffle and an exit riffle and a long reach of water between. They stationed Walter down near the downstream riffle to prevent the salmon from rushing out of the pool toward the sea. Walter stood up to his waist in the river with a long pole, splashing the water to keep the salmon from escaping past him, and the biologists were busy with their count up above. But the salmon spooked, and came down on Walter — according to his story — in a solid black mass, and knocked him down. They were so thick above him that he couldn't get up, he said; he'd start to get to his feet and his head would come up against salmon bellies, and down he'd go again. If the press of salmon hadn't rolled him into shallow water in the riffle he'd have drowned. I suspect that this falls into the tall tale category; Walter was an entertaining storyteller.

Another day Dad and I were taking time out on a freshet-deposited log when a flicker of movement across the river pool caught our attention. A sleek brown otter was humping his way along the shoreline. In one spot, the steepest, the gravel overlay had flaked away from a patch of slick blue clay. The otter arrived at the clay band and started across it. He had almost completed the crossing when his feet shot from under him. He landed on his back with a flourish of stubby legs in air, then tumbled downslope to land in the pool below with an unseemly splash. The otter swam ashore, looked over each shoulder as if to make sure no one had witnessed his pratfall, then made off.

Nature, however, is rarely in playful mood. Oftener than not, the encounters we're privileged to witness are of a darker sort.

One winter day when a scruff of snow covered the frozen earth, another otter that lived in a neighbour's seawall set out for the nearby creek. His dark, streamlined shape was halfway across the white expanse when a bald eagle, turned rash by winter hunger, swooped on him from a Sitka spruce top. There was a wild flurry of flailing wings, reaching talons and snapping jaws. Feathers puffed in a little cloud as the old dog otter, lying on his back now, buried his teeth in the eagle's cushioned breast. The eagle flapped heavily away. The otter limped toward the shelter of the creekside tangles. Behind them, a red splotch on the snow bore witness to this strange and savage encounter.

Eagles are an endangered species in all of the United States save Alaska, but here on this favoured strip of Vancouver Island's east coast, they may be seen during most months of the year. They gather in great numbers in late February or early March, when the herring runs are underway in the Strait of Georgia. Then we see eagles perched on the top limbs of lofty Douglas firs and spruces, eagles wheeling and circling overhead, and eagles by the dozen hulking with snowy tails and fresh-laundered white heads on the boulders that hump out of the low-tide flats.

A school of herring shows up. The swift-flying glaucous-winged seagulls hustle to intercept it. So do the eagles. In seconds, the school's position is marked by a whirling melee of white gull wings and broad, dark eagle pinions as the fowls of the air gather for the feast.

I have wondered more than once whether the eagles stake out territorial rights to the rocks which are their lookout stations. Certainly the eagle that attacked a presumptuous great blue heron was quick to challenge what he obviously regarded as a trespasser. The eagle launched a swift attack. The heron, standing with one updrawn leg and ivory bill resting on breast, rose from the rock and flapped off with skinny legs trailing and crook neck extended. As she oared her way over the shallows, she emitted a series of harsh cries. The eagle stuck with her like an avenging fury. He dive-bombed the luckless heron again and again. One last vicious assault drove the heron into the saltchuck where she floundered to a tune of sepulchral croaking until the eagle, honour satisfied, flew off to take over his rock.

Only once in a long outdoors experience have I been attacked or even threatened by any truly wild creature. The exception came about one day when I was brushing out a fire trail through thick salmonberry cover to a wilderness pond. I took a step forward, swinging my machete, and from around my feet rose a squeaking and a mewing. Instantly, something attached itself to the toe of my logger's boot. I kicked, and a dark creature rather smaller than a house cat went flying. The scurrying and chirring around my feet told the story. I had blundered into a mother mink escorting her brood to the pond, and she had responded in the fashion of all mothers when they fear their young are menaced. Logger's boots are made to withstand all manner of strains and stresses. The toes they protect are shielded by a double thickness of heavy leather. Even so, the mink's teeth had penetrated through the top thickness of my boot toe and dented the layer beneath. In camp I kept the incident to myself. After all, who wants to admit that he was set upon by a lowly mink?

12.

Eastern Exile

Win's HARDY TRIUMPH ROD got its first testing on the Oyster not long before we married. We had joined my father there; I camped with Dad, and Win stayed across the highway at Fishermen's Lodge. One day while I was splitting firewood, Win took the Triumph and started upriver.

An hour or so later, suddenly anxious, I started out to find her. My father came with me. It was he who spotted Win from the highway bridge. She was braced in the first upstream riffle, facing the pool below. Her rod, bent almost double, was whip-sawing this way and that. The first of the year's salmon runs was under way, each pool carpeted with masses of humpbacks, pink salmon as they're called commercially.

"Oh boy!" I said in dismay. "She's snagged a humpy."

Stream law in British Columbia takes a cold view of those who interfere with salmon on their spawning run. To make matters worse, the district game warden had chosen that afternoon for a stream patrol. He was moseying down the bar in Win's direction.

"She'd better break it loose," my father said.

We cupped our hands and bellowed at Win. She heard us over the rush of waters, and flapped a hand in understanding. Then she did everything in her power to free herself from that fish. She hauled back on the rod till it bent double. She whipped it violently sideways. Meanwhile, the warden was only a matter of feet distant.

Finally Win gave a last heave. But its only effect was to bring her fish skittering and splashing into shallow water and thence up the shingle to flap at her feet.

The warden, though, did not reach for his notebook. Instead he nodded his approval, gave Win a smile, and continued his course upriver.

Dad and I hurried down. What we found was no humpy but one of the largest, most beautiful searun cutthroat ever to come our way.

Wordless, we stared at it.

"I tried to get rid of it like you told me," Win said. "But I couldn't figure why on earth you wanted me to!"

Win and I were finally getting married. I went to the *Province* management and asked for a marrying raise—it was almost traditional that you be given one—and the publisher sent word very curtly that he couldn't see his way to giving me a raise. Some of us had tried and failed to bring the American Newspaper Guild in to the *Province*—I held card number three for British Columbia, signed by Heywood Broun—and after that, the management made sure those involved made no further progress. Even when I rated as a senior reporter I think I was getting the princely sum of twenty-five dollars a week. Soon afterward I went east, three blocks east, to work for the Vancouver *Sun*.

Win and I spent part of our honeymoon at Fishermen's Lodge. It was early September, and Dad was camped across the highway in the forestry park. When they weren't fishing, Win and my father would make cucumber pickles in Dad's ramshackle kitchen, then sit down to eat them. They were cronies from the start.

One morning we were astir before dawn. On our way down the river trail, we overtook my father with flyrod in hand.

"There's this place," my father explained. "A stump hole with a nice run below it. That's where they're lying up this year."

We tramped on down. Where the woods were thickest, Win stepped off the brown-earth trail to walk a huge moss-carpeted log that paralleled it. But the green carpet was a snare and a delusion. It masked rotten wood which gave way under my love's feet, dumping her ears over teacup into the pit below.

Win remembers, "I was lying there, not knowing which way was up and wondering if I'd broken something, when I heard a stampede of boots. It was comforting to know that big, strong men were hurrying to rescue me. But they absolutely ignored me. Someone, I think it was my husband, even trampled on me. All they could think of was to recover my precious flyrod. I could hear them checking it over — 'Tip's not broken,' 'Reel's okay,' and so on — while I lay there in a mess of wood-punk. Finally, as an afterthought, they helped me out of the hole."

The first time I enjoyed the hospitality of Fishermen's Lodge, the beer parlour-with-hotel that stood in the shade of massive maples across the highway from the forestry park, I had hiked and hitched my way south from a logging show shut down by fire hazard. Jim and Ma Taylor had the lodge then; while Jim was ostensibly the proprietor, his formidable wife ruled the roost. Ma was kindness itself, but she would stand for no nonsense from the rough-hewn characters who frequented the beer parlour. Let a brawl erupt between a couple of loggers on a Saturday night and Ma Taylor would wade into the melee with swinging broom. They never came too big for Ma. Out they would go to cool their heads and make their peace. Then, when

order had been restored and they had reached a proper state of meekness, they would be permitted to rejoin the revelry.

I had expected to find Dad with his camp set up. But he had been delayed, as I explained to Ma Taylor. Was there a spot where I could sack out? The hotel was still under construction, its upstairs an uncompartmented rectangle all studs and rafters, home to a population of extremely active bats.

"If you don't mind the bats," Ma told me, "You can sleep up there and welcome."

She dug out a cot and grey wool blankets for me. I turned in with the blankets prudently pulled over my head — who wants a coterie of bats flitting about his ears? — and slept so deeply that not even the alarms and excursions of a Saturday night could disturb me.

In time, Jim and Ma Taylor turned the keys over to Percy Elsey, and it was under Percy that Fishermen's Lodge came to full flower. We called him the Mayor of Oyster River. Percy was a small man, close-coupled and spry, with a merry face and a stutter that waxed and waned in direct ratio to the pressures laid upon him.

One late-winter day when I was a reporter on the *Province*, I picked up my desk phone to hear a machine-gun stuttering at the other end of the line.

"B-B-B-Bill" — It was Percy, calling long distance from Fishermen's Lodge — "I'm s-s-s-s-standing here up to my knees in water. The river's f-f-f-f-flooded. If it gets much higher, we're going to l-l-l-l-lose the lodge." An interval of silence, broken only by the humming of the wires. Then Percy's voice again: "G-g-g-g-g-great G-g-g-god, there's a haystack floating down the road!"

How could that be? I wanted to know. Percy, fighting his stutter, explained. The river in wild freshet had broken through to a channel not used for many years. This channel wound its way out to the road a quarter-mile north of the lodge, and the crazy Oyster was pelting down the blacktop, carrying all before it.

What goes up must come down. Presently the waters receded. When next we looked on the river, it was flowing decorously between its banks, with only the ridged bars to tell of past rampages.

Fishermen's Lodge has survived other vicissitudes, fire among them. Through the years, it welcomed any number of anglers to its fried chicken dinners (fried seagull, Percy billed them), its foaming schooners of right Canadian beer, and its upstairs beds where one slept with the river song soothing in his ears.

We were young, we were restless. I had served in the Canadian Army briefly and without distinction. I was in officer training when the army noticed tuberculosis scars on my lungs, probably the legacy of my Swampy Cree childhood, and ejected me. A job as an army censor held no appeal, and the prospect of returning to my old newspaper job — the Vancouver *Sun* at this point — left me cold. So Win and I got rid of our few possessions — excepting our trout gear — and lit out for Toronto. We had a hundred dollars in the kitty, and for travelling companion the flap-eared cocker spaniel, Lucky, who was our family.

In Toronto I checked in dutifully at Selective Service, a despised wartime excrescence, and applied for the permit that would let me hunt a job. From Vancouver? the clerk asked with hauteur. And I claimed to have been a newspaper reporter? He suggested that I call back next Tuesday. Perhaps a spot could be found for me on a provincial weekly.

Disgusted, I took my leave. Win and I left Lucky the cocker spaniel in the care of a kindly waitress, and strolled along University Avenue until we found ourselves in the shadow of the foursquare grey building that housed Maclean–Hunter Publications.

"Bert Lewis works there," I told Win, "from the *Province* news desk. Think I'll go up and say hello."

I left Win in a bleak and tiny waiting room, and entered the warren of brick-lined cells where Maclean–Hunter got out its myriad trade magazines. I spied Bert Lewis with his tie loosened, sleeves rolled up and pencil-laden vest hanging open. Bert gave me a myopic glare, then rushed upon me.

"Am I glad to see you!" he cried, hustling me along by the arm. "We're in trouble," he said. "Our damned Canadian Shipping editor didn't just quit. He sneaked into the composing room and pied all the type for the next issue." Bert propelled me into a cubbyhole of an office. "We have a deadline coming up tomorrow and no magazine. You've got to help me get one out."

I knew nothing about magazine work and next to nothing about Canadian shipping. But here was opportunity. "Sure," I said. "But my wife's waiting out there. I'd better tell her—"

"No time," Bert said. "I'll send someone. Now, start writing cutlines for these pictures."

Six hours later I got back to the waiting room, where I found my love asleep in her chair. I had a job and two weeks' advance pay in my pocket, and to hell with Selective Service.

I was not to see my river again for six years, but this isn't to say that I missed out entirely on trout fishing during our eastern exile. We fished various south Ontario streams with indifferent luck until the day writer-editor Ralph Allen turned up with an artillery map marked in red ink.

He traced a wavering line with a finger.

"That's club water," he told me. Only members would be allowed to fish it. "It's stocked to hell and gone with rainbows." His finger moved to a thinner line, a mere thread of colour that wandered for an inch or two, then vanished. "That's a feeder creek," Ralph said. "I figure some of those rainbows will have moved up into that creek."

The following Saturday we set out to trace down the little lost creek. Even with the map to help, it was like looking for the proverbial needle in a haystack. We wandered among the back concessions from one muddy, potholed road to the next until the morning was well advanced. Still no creek. I suggested to Ralph that we cut our losses, head for the Credit River and try for a trout in such open water as we could find. But Ralph, who had been a war correspondent of high repute, was made of sterner stuff.

"It has to be here somewhere," he said. "Let's keep on a while longer."

We lurched around a bend and across a sketchily planked bridge that clattered under our wheels. Through the interstices I caught the gleam of water.

"This could be it," Ralph said.

He halted his car in a barnyard, where we were approached by a farmer mounted on a tractor. The barn was classic Ontario, red-painted, and the farmhouse in the background was of age-mellowed red brick.

Sure, said the farmer, we could fish in his crick and welcome. Only he ought to warn us we wouldn't catch anything. Used to be trout back in Granddad's day, but all we would find there now was a few suckers.

With a warning to close gates after us, he growled off on his tractor. We set up our rods and tramped across a band of rough pasture to the creek. A big old elm, its roots partially exposed by some past spate, overhung the stream on its far side. A foam island swirled in the deep hole carved among the roots. The creek came down high and murky from morning rain. The prospect was not encouraging.

"Might as well give it a try," Ralph said without much enthusiasm.

I unlimbered a cast. My fly, a silver-bodied bucktail with black-and-white wing, skated down the brisk current to circle the hole. Gold flashed in the dark water, and a lively tug telegraphed itself to my wrist. I was into a fish — and it was definitely no sucker. I skidded it out to the grassy slope. We stared down at a foot-long brook trout in the livery of its kind: vermicular markings on its deep-olive back and fire-spotted circles on its plump flanks. Ralph glanced over his shoulder. "Get it out of sight," he told me. "We don't want that farmer to see it."

That first catch launched us on an afternoon nothing less than idyllic. The stream cleared. The sun came out. It was small-stream fishing as it should be but so rarely is. As we followed its turny-twisty course with a pause to drift a fly down a sunshiny riffle or to search a tar-black pool, one glorious fact grew upon us. This slighted and neglected meadow creek had through the years restored itself until it offered fishing at least as good and probably better than it did in Granddad's day. Its trout—rainbows in the sparkling miniature rapids and jewelled native brookies in its deeply scooped pools—were not large. A foot-long fish was a big one, a fourteen-incher a monster. But they struck freely at both sunken wet flies and floating dry flies and, inspired by the cold water, fought like little demons.

It was mid-afternoon before I remembered the sandwiches Win had put up for me. I poured a shot of thermos coffee and settled my back against an elm trunk.

Dad would love this place and this fishing. I hadn't seen him for years or even thought much about him in the rush and hustle of life in a big city, but now he came back to me strongly. I could see him on the Oyster with his pixie hat pulled down around his ears, or in town of a Saturday night busy with his sermon notes.

His routine never varied. Supper over, he would retire to his cubbyhole of a study. There he would feed paper into his antique Oliver with its type-bar supports perked up on either side like ears, hitch up his chair, and begin in slow and hesitant fashion to compose. As his subject gripped him, he would crouch over his machine, occasionally muttering to himself, while his forefingers beat a rigadoon upon the keys.

In Nanaimo I would wait impatiently for him to make an

end, so that we could get on with the next phase of our Saturday night progression. This was a stroll over the Bastion Street bridge and on downtown, perhaps to return with a treat of fish and chips bundled in a wrapping of grease-spotted newspaper. Or we might walk on past the lighted stores to where an ornate tamale wagon sat on rubber-tired wheels in the shadow of the Anglican church.

There never were or will be tamales as splendid as those evolved by the spry and merry little Mexican who presided over the wagon. Corn-husk wrapped, sizzling hot on the outside from the steamer, and incandescent within from the chilies and spices that flavoured them, they were food almost too good for sinful mortals. My father bought four tamales, one for each of us. Wolfing mine, I would forget the sort of day that lay ahead.

My Sabbath observance would include sitting on a hard wooden pew at morning and evening services while my father delivered the sermons that had burgeoned from his notes. Even in an era when a sermon of an hour's duration was standard fare, my father's sermons were long. At the end of an hour, Dad would be just hitting his stride. Another half hour and my backside would be going numb, while the snowy heads among the congregation would be sagging on their owners' breasts. At the two-hour mark the merely grey heads, and some of the younger ones, would be nodding.

Once my father, carried clean away by his enthusiasm, spoke for a mortal two and a half hours. My mother, taxed even beyond her endless-seeming patience, remonstrated with him. So did my sister Shirley, and so did I.

"You're right," my father admitted. "I've got to do something about this." He turned to me. "Bill," he said, "at tonight's service, I want you to sit in the back row with my watch in your hand. When I've spoken for an hour, hold up the watch. Don't make a big show of it—just hold it so I can see it."

Dutifully at evening service I stationed myself in the rearmost pew. At the end of an hour of sermonizing, I exposed the face of Dad's pocket watch which I held cupped in my hand. If he caught the signal, he gave no sign. His sermon marched on. Half an hour later I repeated the manoeuvre, this time raising a hand with the watch flat against my palm for better visibility.

But my father ignored my signal. There were pastors who cribbed their sermons entire from Spurgeon or other inspired churchmen whose discourses had been collected and published. Dad was not among this number. His sermons were his own, and this one hung on the Mount of Olives, one of his favourite New Testament passages. He spoke on.

In desperation at the end of two hours, I half rose from the pew and, nipping the watch by the end of its gold chain, swung it to and fro like a metronome. That did it. Dad brought his sermon to a bobtailed conclusion. On the way home, he reclaimed his watch.

"Next time," he ordered me, "sit in the front row so I can't miss you."

Dad would like this Ontario creekside, where the sun by now was westering among the trees. I heard the swish of boots in the long meadow grass, and looked up to see Ralph Allen approaching. He wore a grin, and his fishing bag sagged heavily on his hip.

"How'd you make out?" he asked.

For answer, I tipped back the lid of my loaded creel.

"If that farmer knew what we had here," Ralph warned, "this would end in short order. We'd better clean our fish before we get back to the bridge."

This we did, hurriedly and with frequent glances over the shoulder. Then, leaving the innards behind a log for the mink whose dainty tracks we'd seen on the sandbars, we trudged back to Ralph's car. The farmer met us with an indulgent smile.

"Well," he added, "did you catch many suckers?"

We laughed heartily at his joke, hugging our secret to ourselves.

"Matter of fact," Ralph said, "we had a real good day. Nice and warm. Birds singing all over the place." He paused, then said, "You know, you've got a lot of birds here that are kind of rare. We're more bird watchers than fishermen. Mind if we come back for a look at the birds another time?"

The farmer gave his assent. We went back the following Saturday, and the trout were waiting for us. But we had misjudged our man. As we were cleaning our catch, his shadow fell across us. He stared, while a slow grin crept up to hook itself around his weathered ears.

"Well," he said. "Well, now!"

We returned once more to the little lost creek. A sign nailed to a bridge upright greeted us.

"Trout fishing," it read. "Per day, $5.00." The barnyard was cluttered with parked cars, and a glance along the creek's course revealed a fisherman on station at every pool and reach.

With a sigh for lost Arcady, we turned away. It was cold comfort to learn a year or two later that winter floods had scoured the stream bed, and that its now muddy flow was again inhabited only by suckers. Still, I remember that creek fondly for the all-too-brief pleasure it gave us.

13.
He Was Telling Me Goodbye

As TIME PASSED IN TORONTO I yearned increasingly for the sight and the sound, the smell and the touch, of that unruly but beautiful Vancouver Island stream. Occasional letters in my father's angular handwriting did nothing to slake that longing.

"Three channels to the estuary this year," he wrote, and "They're talking about a new highway bridge farther upstream," and "Fishermen's Lodge has a new owner, his name is Charley Chappell, a good man." His homely notes made me realize even more keenly that Win and I were exiles from our rightful land.

For as long as we could hold out, Win and I refused to let the siren song move us. After all, the East had rewarded us beyond our expectations. Lucky the spaniel was long gone, but we had another hostage to fortune in the person of our small son Ron. I had published a serialized novel in the *Saturday Evening Post,* and was selling serials and short stories to top American mass circulation magazines with pleasing regularity. Then one day in a hot and humid Toronto summer, I caught myself dreaming the high-piled cumulus clouds on the Lake Ontario horizon into the snow peaks of home, and knew the only possible antidote to this malaise was a trip to the coast.

We loaded our bags, our cased flyrods and our sleepy little son into a Canadian Pacific Railway compartment on a steamy night when the temperature at ten o'clock stood at ninety degrees. The train pulled out of Union Station. The wheels on the rail joints settled into the clickety-clack that was music to my ears. Their refrain, endlessly repeated, was, "We're going home! We're going home!" It was six inland years since we'd trudged a freshet bar or snuffed the sweet-and-sour tang of log booms in salt water. And it was that long, I realized with a jab of conscience, since I had laid eyes on my father.

Too excited to sleep, I thought about him while the train straightened away on course with half a continent to span. How was he doing? He had given up driving, I knew from one of his letters, and I was glad of that.

Dad had come late to the automobile, and was never truly at home behind a steering wheel. Further, the cars he could afford were not merely secondhand. By the time one of them came into my father's possession, it was about ready for the wrecker's yard.

My father's driving hastened this end. For one thing, he was emphatically nonmechanical. He could never grasp the functions and necessities of the internal combustion engine, with the result that we, or rather I, spend an undue amount of trip-time trudging the highway with fuel can in hand to replenish our gas supply at the nearest garage. He drove as if he were leading a

cavalry charge, crouched over a wheel which he gripped so hard that his knuckles showed white through their tan. To board a car ferry with him was an experience to curl the toes, and the seventy-five-mile drive north from Nanaimo to our river was an adventure with elements of nightmare.

Two flat tires were par for the course. We could also expect to stall on the steeper hills with steam-jetting radiator, and to swoop down their reverse slopes checked only to a minimal degree by brakes that should long ago have been relined. It was my personal conviction that flights of angels guided my father on his erratic way. While he never came to harm, any number of times he shaved the thin edge of disaster.

Once as we clattered along through a recently logged desert of stumps, I noticed that Dad's head was tipped forward and his eyes closed. He had gone fast asleep. Before I could nudge him awake, our ancient Chevy veered off that road, jolted down an embankment, missed one stump, grazed another, and came to rest with its front end nuzzling a third stump.

This interruption Dad took in stride. He started his engine, wrestled it into gear, and threaded his way among stumps until road and logged area were on the same level. Unfazed, he guided us back onto the highway and we resumed our journey.

Another time, we stowed a gallon can of Dad's cosseted worms in the trunk I'd made for the car in high school manual training. Somewhere up around the little town of Bowser — if anything untoward was in store for us it would pounce near Bowser — the side of my ill-crafted car trunk unshipped its moorings and scattered our belongings along a quarter-mile of highway. Dad's precious worms were among the casualties. Naturally, the can took a bounce or two. The lid flew off and Dad's bait supply for our holiday was scattered on the blacktop. We spent the next hour and more ducking in and out of traffic while we rescued such earthworms as we could. Luckily Dad had brought a generous oversupply, of which we recovered only slightly more than half.

One ill-starred day we had two flats in the space of a mile. By the time we had pried first one ragged tire and then a second off its rim, patched the tubes and returned us to running trim, the shadows were lengthening. A few miles farther in our toilsome progress, our headlights dimmed. Undaunted, Dad pressed on. We came to the Big Qualicum River, a stream spanned by one of the typical humpbacked bridges. Dad propelled us up the ramp with engine complaining. A white bulk, dimly seen through the dusk, bobbed ahead of us. Before I had more than identified the object as a cow, we piled solidly into its rear end. The cow bawled, lunged forward, and crashed through the flimsy bridge railing into the river. We scrambled out of the car and hurried to peer through the broken railing. The cow had wallowed its way ashore, and now, apparently none the worse for its misadventure, was fading into the gloom at a laboured trot.

We set off again. Half a mile or so out of Bowser, our headlights gave their last glimmer. This was a situation we'd had to cope with several times before. I dug out a flashlight, and walking ahead of the car, piloted us into a campground on the edge of town. There we bedded down in the mild clear night without benefit of tent. I settled into my blankets with a sigh of relief: sufficient unto the day are the troubles thereof. Surely no more untoward incidents lurked for us.

But later on in the night my father was overtaken by a call of nature. He rose in his white nightshirt and set out lightless to find the outdoor privy. So far, all was well. But not for long. On the return trip, blundering through the darkness of an unfamiliar campground, Dad got lost. He roamed and he wandered, tripping over tent pegs and hanging up on guy ropes. Awake and wondering why he took so long, I heard a subdued shriek. A minute or so later, Dad reappeared, out of breath and cranky, to subside into his blankets. A light flickered in a tent down the line. I could hear voices, one shrill and agitated, the other a sleepy growl. Then blessed silence, which endured until the morning sun was beating down on our faces.

We were making a breakfast of sorts when a man with a worried look traipsed into our makeshift camp. I recognized him as a family acquaintance from Nanaimo.

"Look, Padre," he said to my father. "I wish you'd come and talk to my wife. Try to convince her there's no such thing as ghosts."

"Ghosts?" I asked, startled.

"That's what I said. Ghosts, for pete's sake! She got up to visit the — uh — accommodations last night, and claims she came face to face with a ghost."

Dad, looking slightly sheepish, found something reassuring to tell him.

When the worried husband had returned to his camp, I asked my father, "Are you going to tell her it was you?"

"I certainly am not," Dad said. "Why spoil a good story?"

We loaded our car. With the Ghost of Bowser crouched over the wheel, we continued our toilsome pilgrimage.

Still awake as the train rolled westward, watching a moon-lit countryside glide past our compartment window, I entertained other memories. What my father lacked in driving aptitude, he compensated for by his abilities as a camp cook. Dad had a warmth and a feeling for cooking; he enjoyed his food and took pleasure in preparing it.

His tour de force, his gastronomic triumph, was his Yorkshire pudding. Not the leathery, dark brown popovers that accompany restaurant prime rib dinners but the authentic, magnificent puddings achieved only by cooks with Yorkshire blood in their veins.

To make a Yorkshire pudding on a camp stove was no mean accomplishment, especially since the preliminary step was to produce a roast of beef from the same oven.

A constant supply of even heat was essential. The task of providing this fell to me. Under my father's exacting instructions, I would split a pile of even-sized and not too large pieces of firewood. For the hours which it took to prepare the dinner, I was charged with keeping the firebox stoked with never too much or too little dry wood.

About the time the roast—necessarily a small one—began to give off savoury fragrances, Dad would start his Yorkshire pudding preparations. These were guided by intuition and inspiration.

For a start, Dad would sift a cup-and-a-bit of flour into a big bowl. He would add half a teaspoon of salt. Next he would make a hole in the middle of his flour with a wooden spoon, and break in two eggs if he had them and one if he didn't. He would then add half a cup—or a full cup—of milk to the mix (here intuition played its part) and stir milk and eggs from the centre, introducing the milk gradually until the whole had achieved the consistency of thick cream. Next he would dribble three melted tablespoons of fat from the roast into his rectangular pudding pan which he'd been keeping hot in the oven.

At this point he would give me a stern look and a brusque injunction. "More wood. That oven has to be hot." Finally he would pour his batter into the pan, making sure to tip and tilt it until the corners were well filled.

All this without letting the pan grow cool. Then into the oven with it, where it blossomed gradually from flat white to pneumatic golden brown.

While his pudding cooked, Dad would turn to his gravy making. This was done in the other pan from which the roast had been lifted to keep warm between plates on the back of the stove. Leaving only a couple of tablespoons of fat in the roaster, he would add water from the carrots and potatoes which by a feat of legerdemain had been boiled atop his little stove. He would stir in the tasty black scrapings from the roaster bottom, add a touch of Kitchen Bouquet or any other gravy enhancer he might have, and let his gravy sit over moderate heat while he made another check on his Yorkshire pudding. As a last touch, he pierced each swelling puff with a fork so that it would keep its shape.

The creation that emerged from the oven was a thing of beauty. Its corners stood up like fat little ears. It was light as a summer cloud, so tender that a fork could part it, and when served under a benison of rich gravy, so tasty that the accompanying roast was all but forgotten.

This, my father explained, was the prime function of Yorkshire pudding as served and enjoyed on its home turf. Given generous helpings, the family would stuff so heartily that they'd go easy on the roast, which in such guises as cold plate, shepherd's pie and ultimately stew, was expected to last most of the week.

My father had but two equals as a Yorkshire pudding maker. One was Win's mother, Yorkshire-born in the little heartland town of Market Weighton, who served a peerless pudding. The other is her daughter, my own dear Win, who not only makes a terrific Yorkshire pudding but frequently embellishes it by setting crisp and juicy pork sausages to cruise its billowing surface. This serves as a complete dinner without benefit of roast.

By the time I had envisioned one of Dad's Yorkshire puddings through its evolution to the point where he was serving it — no portions smaller than a quarter of the pan — I was hungry with no food in sight until the train diner opened next morning. With nothing to do but remember great puddings long devoured, I closed my eyes and let the song of the train wheels putting the miles behind us lull me into sleep.

When we checked in at my people's little house in Vancouver's Hastings East, it was to find that my father had aged considerably since we'd last fished a river reach together. His hair, once jet black, was now grey, and he walked with less spring to his step than I remembered. Dad had been away preaching in the interior mountain town of Trail, largely to a congregation of Old Country and Italian miners whom he liked, and who plainly thought well of him. But his war wounds had been giving him trouble, and he was taking an enforced few weeks off to recuperate.

Could he go to the Oyster with Win and me and the small towhaired grandson whom he had met for the first time? I put the question with a sinking feeling that he would be forced to refuse. But at mention of our river, his square face with its cleft jaw, still with its deep-burned African tan, lightened in a smile. He would come, and gladly. Give him a day to put his affairs in order and gather his gear and worms, and he was our man.

So we went up to the river together, me driving us in a rented

car, and checked in at Fishermen's Lodge where the new owner made us welcome. Percy Elsey had taken his stutter and his high-spirited ways to other fields. Big Charley Chappell came after him, a man all kindness with a deep-seated love for children. On our holidays he spoiled our son Ron, and later our little daughter Susan, so badly with gifts and concessions that they became wild as hawks. It took Win and me weeks to bring them back into line.

There had been changes at the Oyster, Charley told us. Advocates of progress—at any price and damn the consequences—had got in their damaging licks. To prevent erosion of bankside land that should never have been sold to private buyers, they had canalized the lower stream almost down to the Willows sea pool, where tidal influence had forced them to stay their hand. With the same idea in mind, a considerable stretch of the north bank above the highway bridge had been rip-rapped with shot rock.

How was the fishing? Gone to hell in a handbasket, I was told, largely through the clearcut logging of upriver woods that had once acted as a huge sponge, feeding water out to the river in gradual allotments. Now all was boom and bust—freshet and drouth—a condition under which fish-viable rivers suffer grievously. The once tremendous winter steelhead invasion had dwindled to a mere remnant of former runs. The autumn salmon pilgrimages that used to lay a wavering dark carpet across the deep of each pool had shrunk to a mere fraction of their former size. Gone were the years when a wading fisherman, caught in a downstream rush of spooked salmon, could be knocked off his feet and all but drowned. How could the searun cutthroat survive? Here Charley became vague. He hadn't heard much about them, but guessed they were mostly gone, too. It was a dismaying prospect.

But that evening I put up a flyrod, pulled on hip boots and took up station near the tail of the bridge pool. The month was September. If any cutties were making their upriver journey, the chances were that I'd find one here.

Without any real expectation I laid out a cast. My bucktail Royal Coachman ducked under and swam deep, a red-white-green confection that searuns found hard to resist. Nothing. No slashing strike, no quick savage pull. I might as well be fishing in a bathtub. Without hope, I dropped the fly a few feet farther down toward the pool tail. Before it could reach proper fishing depth, a cutthroat charged it with a flash of broad, golden side and a swirl that erupted to the surface. I was into the first cutty in far too long. A scene often dreamed of in those six years — years of hurry, scramble and get-ahead — played itself out.

Win came down to the bridge pool seconds after I'd skidded my fish up the bar. I killed it with a tap on the head, and we feasted our eyes on it. Then I hooked a finger under the gill plate and we strolled back to the lodge in the early dusk.

"Where's Ron?" I asked, belatedly returned to a sense of paternal duty.

Win chuckled. "You don't have to worry about him. He and his granddad are sprawled on the floor of our room reading the Sunday comics. At least your father's reading and Ron is peppering him with questions."

In the course of that holiday those two became a familiar sight, strolling the riverbank with Ron's hand secure in my father's, or poking their way along the bars in search of winter-snagged steelhead lures and other such treasures. Once Win and I, estuary bound, paused to watch Dad fording the river one slow step at a time with Ron perched on his shoulders.

"That'd do for a Saint Christopher's medal," I said. But Win didn't answer. She turned away, a hint of sadness on her face, and I knew too well what she was thinking.

Our last day came, as last days must. Autumn was on the land. The lower river flowed diminished between banks carpeted with cloth-of-gold. The salt grass was golden, and so were the leaves of the Pacific willow and tag alder that had sprung up in legions on the freshet bars. In this golden world, my father stood knee deep at the head of the Willows pool. He was letting his spinner flutter down with the current, probing and searching the hotspots with the cleverness and patience learned in his many years on the river.

I saw his rod take a sudden bend.

"Fish on!" he hollered, a familiar and jubilant cry to which the erratic screeching of his reel lent emphasis.

He was into a wild, strong and obviously very large fish. It continued to tear off line, racing downstream for the sea faster than Dad could lumber after it. The end came halfway down the Willows reach. Dad's great cutthroat flung itself above the surface in a leap that rattled its gill plates. Then the rod straightened and Dad was left with trailing line to stare after it.

Dad turned his head. He was grinning. "That fellow," he said, "was telling me goodbye."

On the ferry we stood by the rail and watched Vancouver Island where it lay like a reclining dragon along the western horizon. Win laid her hand on mine.

"I want to come home," she said, and I knew that she didn't mean inland Toronto. "We've been away long enough. You write a serial and sell it and we can move."

"I'll do that," I said.

My father came down to the Vancouver station to see us off. We said our goodbyes, and Dad and I shook hands, but that didn't seem enough. I looked at him standing solidly planted there, a sturdy man with his years upon him, and my throat hurt and my eyes misted. My father, my friend. I put my arms around him and did what I hadn't done since I was a small boy. Hugged him hard and kissed him on his leathery cheek.

Dad was still standing there, looking after us, as the train pulled away. I never saw him alive again.

14.

Bright Waters

DAD DIED THE FOLLOWING OCTOBER. Later, I came on his flyrod. He had been stripping it down with the intention of re-wrapping and varnishing it, a job that I may finish some day. Meanwhile, it hangs in his stained, frayed cotton bag alongside the other rods of my life.

Another two years passed before we got home to the coast. I had written the serial. It had sold. We had put our Toronto home on the market. One June day we got into our car outside a house no longer ours, and pointed our noses west. With us, as well as our son Ron, we had a little new daughter Susan who had never seen the coast.

It is strange how a river can twine its way around a man's life. We live only a mile or two from the Oyster now. We are so close, in fact, that at night from the shore-fronting windows of our house above a Strait of Georgia beach, we see the spaced flashes of Kuhushan Point light which guards the river mouth.

We still fish the Oyster. Thanks in large part to the hard work of the Oyster River Enhancement Society, the salmon runs are beginning to build up again, in a stream not so long ago written off as dead. Partly through the efforts of our provincial fish and wildlife branch, the searun cutthroat are also making a modest comeback. Now we can once again take the trail down to Cutthroat Heaven with hopes of hooking a trout.

My father is one with his river now, but they say a man leaves something of himself in the places he has loved. Often, poking along Willows reach, I'm aware of a presence so real that I glance downstream half expecting to see a stocky familiar figure planted at the next bend. The river was my father's, and he belonged to it heart and soul. Though his corporeal person is long gone, I think some part of him, some vital essence, still lingers by its bright waters.

One blue-and-gold morning last August with the heat devils already dancing above the stony beach, Win and I took the trail to Cutthroat Heaven. Nothing had changed down there. Gaunt weather-silvered drift stumps still offered shade. The kelp bulbs still bobbed brown and shining in the tideway. And, as we'd hoped, the searun cutties were not long in advertising their presence.

Win cast to a swirl, and hooked and duly landed a fine trout. We had brought no lunch and were hungry, so I dressed Win's fish and skewered it on a green sapling trimmed from a wild rose thicket. We built a hot little fire of Douglas fir bark nuggets and grilled our trout over the coals until it was the proper black-brown on both sides. From her jacket pocket, Win produced a paper packet of restaurant salt filed away pawkily for future use. We feasted while the tide crept in over the stones and the sun climbed higher.

"One more cast," I told Win as she scooped sand on our embers with a drift plank end.

The one cast lengthened to a dozen. Then, when I least expected it, a fast-moving hump bulged the surface behind my Mickey Finn. In due time a sixteen-inch searun wobbled on its side in the shallows at my feet. *"Saltavit et Placuit"* was Salome's epitaph, "She danced and pleased." What fisherman could ask for more?

"Shall I keep her?" I asked Win, hoping she'd say no.

Win shook her head. "No need," she said. "Better let it go."

I wet my hands so as not to breach the trout's delicate armour, then cupped her between my palms as I had seen Gypsy Smith do so long ago. For a while I held and steadied her, moving her gently to and fro so that water would circulate freely through her gills. I could feel the life returning to the stream-moulded body cradled in my hands.

Then the lithe and beautiful river sprite was gone with a wiggle and twist and a flip of her spotted tail, back to the freedom of the estuary.

Afterword

One More River

Susan Mayse

A STEEL GREY SEA WAS BRIGHTENING TO BLUE as the sun finally cleared the mountains across the Strait. One small dark figure waded steadily, step after cautious step, into the silver coil of the ebbing tide. Away out in the shallows of the Oyster River estuary, my dad grew smaller and smaller. Finally he was only a black speck on the shimmering water, wading out like a fishing heron, fly casting as he went. Maybe he would wade all the way out to shadowy Mitlenatch Island and never come back.

My big brother Ron was skipping pebbles, and Mum was fly casting inshore. I huddled on the red plaid car rug swaddled in September pre-dawn layers of scratchy wool clothing, piling up all the white pebbles I could seize with three-year-old hands. In that wilderness of tall charred stumps and great salt-bleached drift logs, I was very small. I wriggled a hollow in the shingle and snuggled down in the red car rug. So I drifted to sleep many times, to the silent sweep and return of my father's distant fly casting, or my mother's, and the river quiet.

When I awoke a trout curved silver in the bottom of Dad's net. Mum already had the skillet out of her knapsack and a fire crackling between the logs. Dad squatted on his heels to turn the fish. As the trout's silver skin blackened crisp and curled back from its rosy flesh, a delicate sea scent rose from the skillet. No other breakfast compared with searun cutthroat cooked on the beach. No other freedom matched peeling off one woollen layer after another until noon, then splashing barelegged and salt-crusted through the glittering waves.

At last the afternoon shadows fell on us from the deep forest at our backs. A rare treat of orange Crush in ridged brown bottles fortified us for the long walk back upstream. As we trudged the river trail Dad told us where his father had fished most happily: in the long reach from the bridge down to the river mouth. It was easy to picture him standing, pipe in his mouth and a battered old hat pulled down around his ears, deep in the living stream.

THE RIVER MURMUR RAN THROUGH OUR LIVES, even away back on the furthest bright rim of my memories, the murmur of not any river but this river. Sometimes the four of us piled into the dusty Studebaker to fish Trout Creek away north or little Black Creek a few miles south. We fished Millstream, Duggan Lake, streams in the highlands, streams at Sooke, during our winter sojourns at Arbutus Cove outside Victoria. Always the Oyster River was in our thoughts, coltish in spring freshets or glassy smooth in August low water, our own river.

I don't remember a time when I didn't want to get myself or a fishing line into the nearest water. Splashing mightily, trying the patience of my quietly fishing parents, I was never happier. My first fishing rod was a workaday split cane rod with a plain Scottish reel. Though nearly every other childhood memento is gone, that rod and reel survive from my seventh year. This was my treasure; it allowed me to fish in my own right, and to fish was to merge with the river.

Fishing was our prime reason to return, as habitual as the salmon, to the Oyster River. It was a long day's drive, especially before the Island Highway was finished north of Nanaimo, and on arrival two sleepy children had to be decanted from the Studie. In the early years we stayed at Fishermen's Lodge, where the tame deer would venture into the garden to eat from our hands, and the kindly cook would whip up any treat two small guests might fancy.

Later we stayed at the Chettleburghs' cabins on the south bank of the estuary. Sometimes we camped at Bennett's Point just north of Kuhushan Light or at Miracle Beach. Ron and I spent some envy on friends taken to Disneyland or the Okanagan, the two glamorous destinations for island kids in the fifties. But as we bounced precariously on the flat deck of Terry Chettleburgh's truck over the estuary dunes and through the river ford, kayaked in the bird-haunted swamp, boat fished for salmon, or stream fished for trout, we knew our good luck. In places now commercially developed or protected as parkland, we endlessly swam and fished and played.

Summers ended. Victoria winters seemed long and dark and wet. Storm-driven rain would lash in against our windows at Arbutus Cove, and smoke would beat back down the chimney. Colds and flu stalked the cold weather. When I was sick and frightened and wide awake, Dad would sing me back to sleep. He favoured mournful ballads like "The Streets of Laredo" and "Danny Boy," and the spirituals he'd heard as a boy in his father's church and visiting tent revivals. His inventive tour de force, with endless verses made up for a sick child, was about the animals marching two-by-two into Noah's ark. *One more river, and that's the river of Jordan, one more river. . .* As I floated down into sleep and the birds' dawn chorus tuned up outside, I would see not the unknown desert Jordan but the wooded banks and sunny reaches of our island river. *One more river to cross.*

I never knew my grandfather Will Mayse, since he died three months after I was born. Yet Dad's great love for his father made him a warm presence — rather, a warm tangible absence — in my life. In an often lonely childhood, the grey-haired friends I loved died too soon; relatives were distant. I cried for my granddad. I needed him to speak for me, to be my friend. I hung on stories of his South African adventures and days on the Peguis Reserve.

Will Mayse was one of my childhood heroes. I was surprised, trying on his South Africa uniform jacket as a teenager, to learn how small and slight he had been, this great-hearted man. His life gave me so much: a model of courage and goodness, an origin, a country of my own, a beloved landscape, a river. I was always happy on his river.

Once I asked Dad, as my own little daughter would ask me years later, Where is my granddad now? My answer would in time be my daughter's answer: Granddad was fishing a beautiful river in a far country, as happy as could be. Dad quoted, "In my father's house are many mansions." Seeing that I was confused, he added, "And many rivers." I've always been able to picture Granddad, just as Dad described him fishing the Willows reach on our own familiar Oyster, feet solidly planted and chin tucked down as he waited for a trout.

Arbutus Cove had its own delights. Our gracious white house, at one time a stop on bus tours for its lovely manicured gardens and unusual apple grafts, looked out across the Strait of Juan de Fuca to San Juan Island. Dad's serial *Desperate Search,* later a book and movie, bought the house. At first we occupied it harum-scarum like gypsies; our furniture was an odd collection. Most important, the house had lawns big enough for fly casting practice, cowboy games and training a dog, and a basement big enough for several workbenches.

When I was little Dad would let me help him carve and paint wooden plugs which, like most salmon lures, mimic tasty minnows. Or he would hammer fishing spoons of different sizes from metal scraps and fit them with wire leaders. Plugs usually took wicked treble hooks, spoons took singles. Hanging in a shining row above Dad's workbench were the spoons he had won in a Cowichan Bay fishing derby as a boy. I loved to rub them with brass polish and a scrap of one of my diapers, recently outgrown.

Our beach was a long pebble and sand crescent divided by a small headland we had to scramble over at high tide. This was the family measure of maturity: being allowed to climb the rocks unattended by a parent. We pried and dug and netted all manner of sea life. It was a good clam beach and harboured a few small oysters, the largest mussels I've seen, sand dollars, sea cucumbers, crabs, candlefish, flat fish and migratory salmon.

The beach sheltered generations of rafts and rowboats. Ron's rafts became increasingly elaborate, boasting cabins and masts and bowsprits. My rafts consisted of three or four drift logs three to five metres long, not too waterlogged or splintery, a washed-up hatch cover or beachcombed plywood for decking, and spikes. The Cadboro Bay hardware store did a brisk if highly seasonal trade in five-inch spikes. No challenge quite matched trying to pound a spike through soggy wood with a slippery hammer while CPR's three o'clock steamer waves lurched a ton or two of splintery logs over our bare feet. Our summers were spent with salt-crusted splinter gouges across the brown tops of our feet, and barnacle scrapes across the pale soles. We were tough guys; we knew the raft was everything. Our rafts rarely rode out the fall southeasters, but there was always another summer.

One stormy fall Saturday when Dad was away for a few days and Ron was off with friends, a neighbour phoned to tell us Dad's beached boat was off its logs and afloat. Mum and I went down in a screaming southeaster to see the boat tossed about in a bay churning with huge grey waves that marched in from the Strait. The twelve-foot boat looked tiny. Giant drift logs pitched in every direction like straws as the storm built force, and the spume frothed right up the bottom flight of stairs.

Mum ordered me to stay on the second landing and not move a single inch, and I realized she planned to go down into that frenzied sea. I told her I didn't think it was a good idea, but she climbed down clinging to the handrail. She saw me creep down one step, but her shout was torn away by the wind. The storm's shattering wall of noise was total, destroying all other sound. Then she waded waist-deep among the crashing logs, and somehow managed to haul the boat in by its trailing painter and beach it out of the storm's reach. The boat took a single hole near the stern thwart. Mum could easily have died. She wanted that boat, and she got it.

Winter is catch-up time in a fishing family. Between gales there was always much discussion of tide tables, charts and currents, and much oracular examination of drift logs and flotsam. One year I helped Dad make an old-style herring rake the hard way, by sharpening small finishing nails at both ends and setting them in a needle-toothed row on the edge of a narrow plank. We put the rake to good use in Brentwood Bay, sweeping up bait for bluebacks or early springs. I would sit on a white shell beach with Mum telling me how many millennia it took to grind down a grain of sand or a flake of shell. Her stories covered the creation of rocks and landforms, paleontology, human evolution, and the rudiments of history. A gripping storyteller, she transformed every mundane explanation into a mystery, then solved it for a fascinated child.

Fly fishing lay at the heart of winter preparations for the next season. Dad would go over his gear meticulously — stripping and revarnishing, replacing ferrules and guides and cork, rewrapping silk thread — on his powerful Kohinor or Mum's elegant Triumph. Fly lines were uncoiled and straightened, then returned to the reel. On sunny days I sometimes practised casting with a book held under my arm to keep my elbow down, learning to work out line and bring it in without making a birdsnest. Still, I never really acquired my parents' river sense: where to look, where to drop the fly, how to tease it past the fishy spots, and when to call it a day.

Ideally, an angler ties a fly on the riverbank to duplicate the insects that are hatching or swimming or flying right then and there. In practice some patterns are tried and true for certain rivers, and anglers have their favourites. I remember Royal Coachman and Mickey Finn as Dad's favourites, but these are the bright names and wings of childhood memory. He tied many other patterns sitting on the living room chesterfield at Arbutus Cove with his work board and fly vise on his lap. Sometimes I tied too, though to my critical eye my best efforts looked like fearsome mutations. Dad fished with some of my flies as I still fish with some of his. Elements of his fly-tying kit, now my kit, are doubtless collectors' items. A few were probably his father's gifts after the unsuccessful parrot grab.

Dame Juliana Berners, the American writer Sparse Grey Hackle, Ernest Thompson Seton, even Grey Owl, were the names invoked during these sessions. Izaak Walton and his commentator Charles Cotton stood at the pinnacle of fishing lore. Their slim book had pride of place in the bookshelf, and nearby hung Father Walton's portrait. Roderick Haig-Brown's name was spoken with warmth and respect. Among many other things, all winter we talked of trout and salmon, and trout again. Mum and Dad were great readers, always offering some interesting morsel of archaeology or literature or current affairs. Our talk had a leavening of Chinook Trade Jargon; like many coast people in those days Dad used it liberally. I only realized as I leafed through a dictionary recently how much Chinook I heard at home.

Inevitably, Mum and Dad eventually bought two south-facing riverfront acres above the bridge on the Oyster River. Our property lay on a bend which cradled a long shadowed pool darting with real and fancied trout. A venerable cottonwood tree overhung the top riffle; the exit riffle sparkled out into clear sunlight where a logjam and backwater opened the tree canopy.

One shining summer we camped there for a few weeks. We bushwhacked out a trail with the machete, dug a latrine, pitched the green umbrella tent, hung a tarpaulin fly, nailed a mirror to a tree, and were home. Every afternoon, once Dad and Mum had finished their morning fishing, it was my turn to swim. I floated and splashed in the pool from mid-morning to evening, sunning occasionally on the sandbar. Later we would all fish the evening rise. It was high summer, when the cottonwood and alder leaves turned silvery dry, and the river was blood warm. I would hang in the current for hours at a time, holding my place in the flow by grasping a projecting cottonwood root, watching the dappled clouds float high above and the first falling leaves float on the river's reflected sky, slowing down and down until I was a trout, I was the river.

That summer from a boat we fished the violet evenings from Kuhushan south past Oyster River to Black Creek. Fishing annulled all our domestic frictions. We shared our potato chips and regretted their saltiness after the juice or coffee was gone. Mum made up fish songs, alternately threatening and cajoling salmon to leap over the gunwales. Dad's big blunt hands would fuss with the tackle, tying and trimming and repairing with improbably delicate skill. Over the purr of the small outboard motor our human silence was friendly, and our talk rested as easily on the best leader length for bucktails as on the nature of life. It was an occasion repeated often with minor variations, perhaps a family of dolphins playing around the boat or an unexpectedly hooked crab.

When twilight darkened the Eagle and the Ice Cream Cone, as we called two of the Coast Range mountains, when the sea was gun-metal blue under the light cross-chop of an offshore breeze, when the last sunset light illuminated little Mitlenatch Island like the sea-going saints' golden island in the west, it was time to haul in our gear and run for home. In our upstream camp in the cottonwood's night shadow we would fry up cold potatoes with onions, fish if we'd caught them, and maybe steam some sweet corn. If we were down to corned beef Dad, like his father, would fry up a hash.

At last we packed our tent and rolled our bags with great plans for next summer: an open cook shack, a better trail, a tarpaulin-wrapped latrine with a river view. The capricious river decided otherwise. Its next freshet straightened our bend, scoured the lovely pool down to its bed and swallowed a third of our property. The Oyster was always a wild and wandering river, as a glance across its broad floodplain reveals. Mum and Dad decided to sell while some land still remained to sell. Our golden summer was, after all, our last summer upriver.

The peace and fullness of those drifting days have eluded me ever since. Every river I measure against the Oyster; every bend and pool I measure against our pool. In all the years I have found few places to match this beauty.

Difficult years came for all four of us as Dad's markets for the short stories went under one by one: *Collier's*, *Country Gentleman*, *Liberty*, finally even *Saturday Evening Post*. Dad had been a phenomenal success among Canadian writers: skilled, respected, in demand by the world's foremost fiction markets, able to live comfortably. Suddenly we were poor, and no one knew Dad's name or wanted to buy his work. Later Dad told me of his deep depression and thoughts of suicide, and Mum's decision to keep him alive. Years earlier one of their Oyster River friends had come home to the coast bent on suicide after a dreadful war experience. His wife took him to a handliners' camp upcoast where their only concerns were to haul salmon, sell to the packer, eat and sleep. Her wisdom saved his life.

On the coast, hard-hit by the Depression and Second World War, there were many such survival stories. That summer Mum dragged Dad out salmon fishing every evening, week after week. They would come in after dark like a pair of school chums, arm in arm, laughing and salt-splashed, with some fish story to tell. Dad went back to newspapers, writing features and columns for the Victoria *Times*.

I clung to my world with an instinctive knowledge of

childhood's impending end, and long after my classmates were immersed in movies and dates and clothes, I was living out my coast dream. One summer I took out a Class B troller licence, when a rowboat handliner could still do so, and fished. Dad and I rebuilt the rowboat he had made for Ron, sprung at bow and stern transoms by an unseasonable gale, now mine for ten dollars.

Seal, eight feet long, became one of the coast's smallest trollers. My hand-painted regulation numbers stretched almost from waterline to gunwale. I worked at fishing sporadically, but spent most of my time rowing lazily or lounging on the floor-boards as I drifted with tide, wind and current between Gordon Head and Ten Mile Point. A summer breeze tickled overhead, dolphins and seals frolicked around seakind *Seal's* motorless hull, and frustrated gulls occasionally dropped a clamshell they wanted to crack on the thwarts. I saw ling cod as long as my boat, spider crabs, the busy marine life on a reef where I liked to anchor, cormorants in their cliff face nests. Each creature was in its element, and I in mine.

I had everything but fish. The coho that year, it turned out, ran the other side of Vancouver Island. I was only mildly disappointed. By fourteen I had already decided to fish, in the saltchuck or on rivers, not against the fish but with them. If they offered themselves to the hook I was happy to land, gut and eat them. But if the fish were feeding as lazily as I was fishing, or if they rightly concluded my fly was a plot against their lives, I was even happier to stand quietly knee-deep in a sunlit river enjoying my world.

Four years later I saw fish, countless thousands of fish, from a different perspective on the packing line and scaling tank of a Victoria salmon cannery. As run after run came in we processed humpbacks, coho, spring and sockeye. We cleaned the freshest and prettiest fish for the Chicago fresh fish market or the freezer fish market. The rest we canned.

Canners could be fresh sweet-smelling fish with the sea lice still clinging around their vents, well cleaned on boats with plentiful ice — or they could be round or ungutted fish kept for days in iceless holds. These, when the two cutters butchered off their heads and tails and ripped their guts, sent up a powerful stink. We soon learned to ask as every boat nudged the bumpers on our dock, "Clean or round?" Some of the ripest fell apart in our hands, and many more were riddled with maggot eggs. Somehow the eggs blended invisibly with the salmon once it was steam-cooked in the big vats. It's all protein, shrugged the cannery hands.

It was a wonderful adventure, after an isolated and eccentric upbringing, to encounter the real working world of commercial fishing: the fish, the cannery workers, the government inspectors, the boats, the fishermen. We worked full shifts, then time and a half overtime, then double time overtime, straight through from mid-June to mid-September without a day off. Every day I got up early, drove through the vibrant morning smell of gardens and lawns to the stale miasma of the canning floor, worked until my arms were ready to drop off, stumbled home and fell into bed. While the rest of Canada was visiting Expo 67 and celebrating Canada's first century, our canning line clattered and steamed like the country's true working heart.

Nowhere on the face of the earth did I want to be more. I was living my coast, earning my stake in *illahie*. In the blunt spare Chinook trade jargon, depending on context *illahie* may mean the ground underfoot, a handful of soil, this place, this property, this country, this earth. For me it always meant this coast.

Dad understood, reluctantly, when I left to work in the Northwest Territories after university and marriage. Mum, a hard-headed business woman, needed no explanation. Before we caught our plane north, I took Stephen up island for a last walk by my river. In Yellowknife I thought I would die outright of homesickness. Mum and Dad sent boxes of golden delicious apples from my favourite tree, boxes of fir bark and split alder for the best fire, and a splendid Cowichan sweater. We planned to be away a year, then return with job experience to the island. Who would want to be anywhere else?

Everywhere I moved, I took *Seal's* worn brass oarlocks and my flyrod. Year after year, there was always one more adventure ahead, one more river to cross. By chance we saw the ice pack break out of the great Mackenzie one June day with the grinding roar of two trains colliding. At First Canyon on the Nahanni, in the temperate microclimate of hot springs surrounded by permafrost and muskeg, Stephen stood guard with a .303 while I soaked in a warm mudhole a stone's throw from the furious grey river. In northern lakes that from the air looked like scattered glass beads, we trolled for deep-bellied lake trout. We fished glacial waterfalls for lively Arctic grayling, and fished lakes from the pontoon of a float plane. We caught bony northern pike—the dogfish of the north—and ate them. Once by candlelight in an isolated Dene settlement three of us shared one potato, which was all the people could spare us from their meagre supplies, and a northern pickerel we were lucky to catch. Nothing ever tasted better. We moved to Edmonton for a year, and stayed sixteen. I was long over my homesickness. Raven River, North Saskatchewan, Sturgeon, nameless streams of the mountains and foothills, Athabasca, Peace, Oldman, Battle, Red Deer and Bow: we fished some, canoed others.

On the island, Mum and Dad took their opportunity in the early seventies to move nearer to the Oyster River. They bought Cecil "Cougar" Smith's house among the salt grass and sea oats on Stories Beach from Mrs. Smith, his widow, and moved in a year later. From the gracious house on Arbutus Cove they moved to a tiny shingled cottage bought with cougar bounties. It had started life as a floating bunkhouse at a logging company's beach camp far up Toba Inlet, and under the foundation skirting it still rested on its huge skids. These were the logs on which it had floated down inlet and had been winched up onto Stories Beach.

When Dad and Mum undertook modest renovations, one of their first discoveries was a pack of playing cards hidden under a window framing stud. The pack had five aces.

Stories Beach was their whimsical choice of variant spellings for the long shingle and sand curve north and south of Stories Creek. Storey was the name of the family who settled the area, but Mum and Dad made their living from stories, so why not? Stories Beach lies three miles north of Oyster River. Here Mum and Dad were only minutes away from the stream that had played such an important part in their lives. Better still, they discovered that they had a pocket version of Cutthroat Heaven about ten paces from their back door. They could, and often did, venture out first thing in the morning to cast a fly from their shingle beach and five minutes later have a cutty or two in the skillet for breakfast.

Dad continued writing one column a week for the Victoria *Times*, later the *Times-Colonist*. His many loyal readers, of all ages and backgrounds, faithfully followed his and Mum's travels and daily doings. His clear prose was an invitation to any reader, however humble or sophisticated, and a great warmth and wisdom shone out from his columns. People read with wonder and amusement of the battle to keep Stories Creek within its banks in spring spate, the intriguing collection of friends and acquaintances, the vigil to ensure winter high tides didn't creep into the living room, the time the neighbour's pig ran away, and many splendid fishing expeditions with or without a harvest of fish.

One of Dad's favourite tales featured his proud construction of a smokehouse. Mum, out to admire it, asked mildly if it wouldn't be easier to put in trays of fish if it had a door instead of four walls. Her smoked salmon was the ultimate fish experience: as hard-smoked as Indian smoked salmon, in no need of refrigeration, but more flavourful because of her brining recipe for soaking the salmon chunks overnight before smoking. Once while they were smoking a new batch, a large car with

United States plates pulled into their gravel drive. The driver said helpfully, "Sorry to trouble you folks, but your privy's on fire."

Best of all people liked Dad's loving kindness toward Mum in the columns and in person. With no hint of derision he called her his mousie, his sweetie and his dear one. One of his readers once wrote that her husband had found a younger mousie and no one now called her dear one. Dad kept her letter, somehow poignant instead of maudlin, for years. His warmth and kindness were genuine, and extended far beyond the printed page. Strangers have told me how Dad helped them find work, sponsored their education, gave them money, succoured them through the valley of the shadow. He was his father's son.

In 1987 Dad wrote to remind me that *Seal* was weathering away on his beach, no longer seaworthy. Finally we flew home to give her a Viking funeral, a great beach blaze that popped her layers of paintwork and sent a column of smoke high into the sky. Dad asked me often, increasingly often as years passed, when I was coming home to stay. He said, "You belong to the coast."

Far rivers still tempted me—Thames, Liffey, Clyde, Seine, Welsh mountain streams with names set to music—and every stream I crossed led to a new territory, a new awareness. I began to see the smallness of my understanding. Colorado, Rio Grande, Pecos, rivers of the high plains and shortgrass prairie, ghost rivers of dryland canals, desert springs: at some point in these journeys I learned to love the minimalist landscape of open country that stretches mile after mile, teeming with small-scale miracles for those who look. I understood at last that this place was home, that all places were home.

Over the years Dad and I fell into the habit of exchanging manuscripts, advice, moral support, criticism and praise. At first I was the one asking advice and accepting encouragement; after my first book was published the exchange became more equitable. When he called early one summer to ask me to read his new manuscript, I asked whether his new book was another juvenile novel like *Handliner's Island*. This was something different, he said. "I'm not sure quite what it is, truth to tell."

His hesitation made me uneasy. Dad always had a clear sense of market niches, and a master angler's skill at casting his stories into their murky pools. This book was about rivers, he said, or perhaps about one river, or perhaps about his father . . . Would I have a look? Maybe I'd know what it was, and what he should do with it.

My Father, My Friend turned out to be a deceptively small and simple book, a sunlit book written straight from the heart with all the craft of an accomplished storyteller. I began reading with special attention, eager to know more of my granddad. I'd already heard some of the anecdotes, and some were new. I finished and phoned immediately to tell Dad I liked it, and to thank him for giving me back my granddad. Dad had long since decided I was a hard case, unsentimental and detached. Both of us were profoundly startled when I started to cry. So did Dad. It fell to Mum, the businesswoman, to take the phone and tell me this was Dad's best book, written with a lifetime's love and longing.

Dad came back on the line to explain the book's genesis. He had set out to write a magazine article for one of the outdoor magazines to which he contributed, perhaps *B.C. Outdoors* or *Outdoor Canada* or *The Flyfisherman*, about the trout rivers he had fished. As the pages mounted beside his old Olympia manual typewriter, he realized his piece was longer than an article. He'd only written about the one river he loved most, and his story had been hijacked by the man he loved most.

A less experienced or less courageous writer would have wrestled the article back to its intended topic. Dad knew how to stand back, as he described the process, when the people in a story took on their own life and started running things. This ability was always his delight and his virtuosity as a fiction writer, but the present venture wasn't fiction, and — after decades of crafting stories easily, lightly and deftly—he found this writing difficult and bitterly painful. It brought back many memories, some bleak, some sunny. In the end, its writing gladdened his heart.

That winter, on the spur of the moment, I flew to Campbell River. Three days later I was walking the river trail to the Oyster River estuary. We had decided to fish the early tide that morning, but six o'clock seemed unreasonable when it arrived. Over pancakes Dad said patiently that it would be all right if we got there by nine. Just one little stop in Campbell River, I promised, to pick up new waders. My old ones had perished. We got to the river at eleven. Dad was resigned. "No point fishing now, sweetie. Let's just take the walk to Cutthroat Heaven."

As we walked Mum pointed out some of the huge stumps from hand-logging days, with their springboard notches for the fallers high over our heads. Elsewhere such giants fell before bulldozers to make room for marinas and malls and sub-divisions, but James MacIvor's old homestead is now a Strathcona-Comox Regional District park. The maples I remember as lithe young trees were themselves giants now. Dad's angina forced him to walk slowly. We rambled along the boundary of the University of British Columbia experimental farm, then back out to the river trail, now marked as the Ferguson Trail and MacIvor Trail. Among the willows, Dad said he'd always wished this favourite stretch of his dad's could be called The Padre's Walk.

Where the Oyster reaches the sea, the river trail follows the university farm fence northward among wind-blasted cedars and firs. It nears the beach again where a down-log offers a natural bench with a view south past Black Creek toward the Comox peninsula. There the three of us sat in a companionable row, Dad catching his breath, Mum and I counting eagles. Before we walked on we took snapshots, two by two, all of us smiling just to be at the Oyster mouth and together. On the way home we warmed up over draft beer at Fishermen's Lodge, marvelling over the longevity of the cased Alaska king crab, the mounted steelhead and cutthroat. Mum asked, Do you remember the tame deer? It was familiar territory, close to home.

A few months later Stephen and I came home to stay. The prairie rivers fell behind us one by one until we reached the divide where all rivers run west. Here my car died, putting sentimentality in its place, and had to be coaxed and rolled most of the way down to tidewater.

We spent two hectic years in North Vancouver, producing between us three books and a daughter. Dad sent a light-hearted welcoming poem for Heledd:

Welcome, welcome, little trout,
Welcome on your coming out.
May Mum and Daddy treat you well
(If they don't, we'll give 'em hell).
May your days be glad and bright,
May you soundly sleep at night.
Baby we have yet to see,
Prosper like the green bay tree.
Grow in beauty, grow in grace.
We love you, little funny face!

Heledd was six months old when I talked Dad into a salmon fishing trip off Kuhushan Light. I'd asked him for years to make me one of his skookum bamboo rods, but he could no longer buy good quality bamboo rod blanks. For Christmas they'd given me a store-bought salmon rod and, perhaps in a fit of madness, a Hardy salmon reel. We went out one beautiful late summer evening, a little early in the year for bucktailing but about right for a small spoon and dodger. Dad and I trolled in his yellow aluminum runabout north to their house at Stories Beach, south past Oyster mouth to Black Creek's lovely unspoiled estuary, north again.

As the evening deepened, Dad pointed out the dark hump

of Confederation Ridge where all those years ago he'd seen the Sayward Fire crown at unbelievable speed, racing south toward the little towns of Bevan and Cumberland, where we now spent our summers. Now the ridge was thick with second growth. We talked about the depredations of the logging companies, how they'd changed from the small family operations of Dad's day, how they'd lost his trust and respect. We settled family business. We talked of books. His juvenile novel *Handliner's Island* and my biography *Ginger: The Life and Death of Albert Goodwin* had come out almost simultaneously, and both appeared in Harbour Publishing's spring 1990 catalogue. This delighted me; Dad was doubtful.

"I don't want to steal your thunder, kid."

"Think you can?" I grinned.

Dad did a satisfying double-take, and grunted, "Guess not."

A halfhearted strike, a line strung with seaweed after a tangle with an offshore kelp bed, a try at hauling out more line, another turn south. Then a coho struck my spoon with gusto, and took off for Mitlenatch Island, which lay tawny gold in the late sunlight. The Kwagiut called it the island that grows no closer for its deceptive proximity. Dad cut the motor and reeled in his own line, and we drifted on the blue mirror of evening slack tide while I played my fish. Dad netted it at last, a gleaming deep-sided six pounder just right for the barbecue. We had talked, solved the problems at hand, contemplated the nature of life, and caught our salmon. It was time to turn for home.

A year later Stephen and I decided to make the last crossing home, and put our house up for sale. Heledd belonged to the coast too, and North Vancouver was only nominally the coast. Then Dad phoned, badly shaken, to say that Mum had suffered something like a stroke and was in hospital. He needed us.

Hospital corridors swallowed all our lives for six months, but especially Dad's. For long months we tried to sell our house and get home. Mum's speech and mobility were severely damaged; Dad tired increasingly easily. Each of them worried constantly about the other. Moved by their devotion, the nurses and supervisors became their warm extended family. Dad ignored warnings about his angina and visited Mum every day from morning to evening. He didn't break the rules for visiting hours, exactly. Rules broke on him, and changed direction to flow around him.

Sometimes the nurses let him catnap on an empty bed. Once I came in and found them both on Mum's bed, two white heads side by side on the pillow. When the nurses finally chased him out, he would drive the seven miles south to the house at Stories Beach where he never gave up hope that Mum could return. His doctor counselled realism and acceptance; Dad politely told him to buzz off. In the dark winter evenings he would fry up a camp dinner and settle by the fire with one of his favourite outdoor catalogues, thumbing over the rods and tackle, windbreakers and walking shoes, planning for summer.

At last we arrived in Cumberland in a whirlwind of boxes and bundles. We took Dad for a Valentine's Day supper after visiting hours in Campbell River. Dad gave his only granddaughter a red satin-covered heart-shaped box of chocolates. Heledd was suitably impressed, and gave a chocolate to her Taid. Not yet two, she couldn't pronounce Granddaddy well, so we'd settled on the easier Welsh word. Dad never courted children or cats, but both would seek him out and demand his attention. He taught generations of kids to fish and tie trout flies and handle a boat. He and Heledd quickly became great friends.

A few days later Dad sat up in his armchair all night while his fireplace logs fell to ashes, unable to sleep because of chest pains. In the morning he phoned his friends, Mum's nurses, to explain why he'd be late. Horrified, they told him he was suffering a heart attack, and sent an ambulance. For a month Mum and Dad occupied adjoining wards. The nurses made sure they had their daily visits.

Nearer now in Cumberland, I visited most evenings, sometimes with a sleepy girl in my arms. Dad sometimes absent-mindedly called her Susan. Heledd, worried, tried to cheer her Taid. One evening she danced like a little flame for him, portraying every creature she could think of: bumblebee, raccoon, whale, otter, salmon, seagull, cat, cougar, deer, bear. Dad loved Heledd's sunny spirit and especially admired her eyes, light and dark blue like the shallows and pools of his river. Dad told me he'd already picked out a flyrod for Heledd, and was planning her first expedition to the Oyster River. He would teach her to fly fish, and tie flies, and carve her first willow whistle from a sappy spring branch. He would carve her a yew shortbow in the hope she would do no more harm with it than I had with mine. I told him how much I needed him. Heledd needed him more.

"Don't be too sad, sweetheart," Dad told me one evening. Mum was failing, as even he finally understood. I worried that he would relinquish his own life in sorrow. But they had made a pact, Dad told me. If one of them died or was incapacitated, the other would live to the full for both. Mum told him once, with difficulty, "We have to live each day now. No past, no future." Maybe it was time to leave Campbell River; hospital beds and services were more complete down island. Dad asked me to bring real estate flyers, and decided he'd try Sidney. It was a good place for an old trout, and Mum could get a bed in a nearby hospital. He told me, just in case, that they both wanted their ashes scattered at the mouth of Black Creek. It was one of their favourite haunts, not developed like the Oyster but as wild and beautiful as always.

Dad was cheerful when sleepy Heledd and I visited just after her second birthday. I was tired and downcast. My car needed work. We wanted to build on our gulf island lot, but weren't convinced. I despaired over the irreversible environmental damage, the crime, the blighting of children's joy and imagination by schools, the diseased society. Dad thought about all this in his usual silent way, and said, "Maybe you'll find what you need on your island."

Maybe, I conceded. It was two days before the spring solstice. Out of darkness, light. Out of death, life. Right now I needed green growing things, bedding plants and seeds. Dad, always a careful gardener, approved. We talked about the old apple trees in my garden at Cumberland, and the old-fashioned flowers and herbs that generations of miners' families had planted around their company house, knowing that strangers would reap what they sowed. It was time to plant again. We said our usual goodbyes, exchanged our usual kiss. Heledd had fallen asleep on my shoulder, but Dad kissed the top of her curly head. I went off, more optimistic than I'd arrived, to plant my garden.

Stephen found Dad as excited as a boy when he visited the next day. A contract had arrived from Harbour Publishing for *My Father, My Friend*. Everyone there who'd read the manuscript was enthusiastic. He couldn't wait to hash over the details of the contract with me.

Later, in the small hours, the doctor phoned to say that Dad had died of a massive heart attack. A few days later Heledd said, half-asleep, "Taid is happy now. Nana will be happy soon." Mum, knowing her loss, died two weeks after Dad.

Letters and phone calls flooded in. Eulogies appeared in newspapers. Somehow we stumbled through the committals and memorial services, the kindness of friends and strangers. Mum was liberated from a terrible half-life, but our loss of Dad at the same time was unbearable. Somehow we celebrated their remarkable lives. Somehow we rejoiced that they had escaped their pain and sorrow as they wanted, together.

In the midst of all this, dazed with grief, I was also seized by panic. Over the years Dad had told me so much wilderness lore, history and family tradition, knowledge of wind and water, the ways of fish and wild animals. His memory was keen to the end. Better than most people living he had known the coast, its distant and recent past, its creatures, its places, its people, its needful skills and knowledge. I had used Dad heedlessly as my personal database, asking and forgetting, asking and never thinking to write his answers down. Now our only treasure was lost, we had lost our storehouse of wisdom and knowledge. Who would ever tell me anything again about *illahie*? Who would teach Heledd to fish? Who would make her first willow whistle?

Finding the fishing rod Dad had picked for her became a compulsion. I combed the stores in Campbell River looking for the child's flyrod he had seen. Store owners and clerks were kind, but they hadn't seen Dad since last summer, and he'd said nothing then about a flyrod. Maybe a little spinning rod would do? But I wanted the rod he'd chosen, I needed it. The rod, and the silver killer whale brooch he'd asked me to pick out for her second birthday, were all Heledd would now have of her Nana and Taid. Then I remembered how Dad had spent his long lonely evenings after hospital visiting hours: poring over his fishing books and well-thumbed catalogues. In one of them I found a lovely scaled-down fly outfit with a rod case, graphite rod, graphite reel, line, leader, even a flybox full of flies. It now waits in her closet until she's a foot or two taller.

A willow whistle was harder. I never had been any good at willow whistles. Stephen brought me a willow branch, not from Stories Beach or the Oyster, but from high in the Tsable River country above Cumberland. I left it to soak for a few days in a glass of water, then cut off a handspan length, carefully ringed the bark at the top and tried to slip it off. No luck. By my third try, tears were dripping down my knife hand and making every-thing harder. Finally I cheated, slit the bark to gently peel off the top thumb's breadth, cut away a wedge and replaced the bark with the help of crazy glue. The thin springtime peep of the whistle, like the cry of a fledgling robin, enchanted Heledd. It was enough.

Dad's other lore is not wholly lost either. My panic abated

as I realized how much of it I applied every day: reading tide and current, running a boat, tying knots, hilling potatoes, taking up awl and beeswax to repair a shoe, writing a letter in Chinook. Much more knowledge resides in Dad's many books, short stories, dramas, articles and columns published and broadcast in his sixty-plus years as a writer.

One raw spring day the three of us smuggled a fir seedling in a nursery pot and an army surplus trenching tool into the Oyster River park. There was no shortage of trees there, but Dad's minister Peter Parker had given Heledd a seedling to remember her Taid by. The mystery of life's renewal may have eluded Heledd, but she threw herself eagerly into this strange expedition. The place she picked for the little tree was at Cutthroat Heaven, out of the wind but in sight of the sea. Nearby was the down-log where Mum and Dad and I sat chatting about eagles only a blink or two ago. We hid the spade and tried not to act guilty when anyone passed us on the trail. Heaven knows what they thought we were planting.

We scattered Mum's and Dad's ashes at the mouth of little Black Creek one peaceful July evening at the turn of the tide. The sun had set behind Confederation Ridge, but the saltchuck and Mitlenatch Island were still bright. Ron and I mixed the ashes in Mum's blue garden pail and scattered them in handfuls. Perhaps the searun cutthroat thought there was a sudden hatch of some unknown insect; with every appearance of delight they rose in swirl after swirl across the shallow estuary as the ashes drifted toward the open sea.

WILL MAYSE DIED POOR, AS HE LIVED, but at peace. He died care-worn, tormented by war wounds, less than happily married, unemployed and without savings at sixty-eight, living with his daughter Shirley, gently declining help from his son. Dad used to say that our family curse was not the aristocratic *noblesse oblige* but our own perverse *oblige sans noblesse:* an obligation to serve, regrettably unmatched by material resources sufficient to make service comfortable.

If we live in our good works after we die, then my granddad is still a benevolent presence. In editing Dad's book I found myself reflecting often on his goodness. Will Mayse practised goodness almost exclusively for the benefit of others; the one kindness he habitually did himself was visiting the Oyster River. In many ways, including his goodness, other lives parallel his life. Dad grasped that the specific chronology of his father's life, the details, are insignificant. His goodness and its effect are most important. Sometime after his dismissal from Vancouver Heights Baptist Church, Dad wrote a sonnet for his father:

> It was no church for him. He was too fine,
> Too far above that thrill-desiring crew.
> They planned, behind his back, for someone new.
> He cast his pearls to something less than swine.
> One could have laughed had it not been so sad
> To see him stand, the lonely dreamer there
> Preaching, or with his tired face raised in prayer
> Fighting for souls where no souls might be had.
>
> I think Christ came into our church that night
> When the late spring flamed sweetly into June
> And white-winged moths danced blind out of the moon
> To beat their wings against the hard, hot light,
> For he spoke strangely at his sermon's end
> As if to greet some well-beloved friend.

Will Mayse left as his lasting work a life of loving service. When we forget him, when we forget anyone like him, we are all poorer. This is Heledd's inheritance, but it flows deeper and broader than blood alone; it is everyone's inheritance.

Heledd and Stephen and I return whenever we can to the Oyster River, sometimes to fish but more often to walk and reflect. Rising in its high country, flowing through its confluences, bends, pools and riffles, mingling finally with tidewater, this will always be our river. And away south in our own small corner of *illahie* I sometimes sing to Heledd, who will make her own crossings, *One more river, one more river to cross.*